GATEWAY SERIES

THE FAREWELL ADDRESS OF GEORGE WASHINGTON

EDITED BY

FRANK W. PINE, M.A.

ENGLISH MASTER, THE HILL SCHOOL, POTTSTOWN, PA.

NEW YORK .:. CINCINNATI .:. CHICAGO

AMERICAN BOOK COMPANY

G. Washington

PREFACE BY THE GENERAL EDITOR

THIS series of books aims, first, to give the English texts required for entrance to college in a form which shall make them clear, interesting, and helpful to those who are beginning the study of literature; and, second, to supply the knowledge which the student needs to pass the entrance examination. For these two reasons it is called *The Gateway Series.*

The poems, plays, essays, and stories in these small volumes are treated, first of all, as works of literature, which were written to be read and enjoyed, not to be parsed and scanned and pulled to pieces. A short life of the author is given, and a portrait, in order to help the student to know the real person who wrote the book. The introduction tells what it is about, and how it was written, and where the author got the idea, and what it means. The notes at the foot of the page are simply to give the sense of the hard words so that the student can read straight on without turning to a dictionary. The other notes, at the end of the book, explain difficulties and allusions and fine points.

The editors are chosen because of their thorough training and special fitness to deal with the books committed to them, and because they agree with this idea of what a Gateway Series ought to be. They express, in each case, their own views of the books which they edit. Simplicity, thoroughness, shortness, and clearness, — these, we hope, will be the marks of the series.

HENRY VAN DYKE.

THE editor wishes to thank his friends and colleagues, Mr. Howard Bement, Dr. John A. Lester, and Mr. George D. Robins, for their valuable help in editing this book.

F. W. PINE.

THE HILL SCHOOL.

INTRODUCTION

LIFE OF WASHINGTON

I. Ancestry and Parentage

George Washington was descended from a long line of English-Norman ancestors, a successful, thrifty race, knights and gentlemen of the manor of Sulgrave in Northamptonshire, England.

John Washington, his great-grandfather, emigrated to Virginia in 1658, and settled at Bridges Creek in Westmoreland County. He was a royalist, and left England because of the ascendancy of Puritanism under Cromwell. Of Washington's father, Augustine Washington, we know little. He was an affectionate husband and father, and a quiet man, who found his pleasures in the care of his estates. Washington's mother, Augustine's second wife, was a gentlewoman of austere demeanour and few words. She was imperious and accustomed to be obeyed. After the surrender of Cornwallis, Washington stopped, on his way north, at Fredericksburg to see his aged mother. When she heard he was at the tavern, she commanded the servant to "go and tell George to come here instantly," and he obeyed the summons. However, she was a loving mother, who retained the affectionate regard of her illustrious son to the end of her long life.

II. Boyhood

George Washington was born on February 22, 1732, at Bridges Creek, Virginia. We owe much to his later biographers, who have helped dispel the popular illusions regarding Washington's boyhood. Stories like those of the cherry tree and the training of the colt disguised the real boy with a priggish and unnatural character that weakened the value of the great leader's life as an example to his countrymen. There is no evidence that Washington, as boy or man, ever made a show of his truthfulness. In fact he was a natural boy, strong and lively, fond of outdoor life, and skilled in physical exercises. He was industrious as a student, not particularly bright, but careful, exact, and persevering. His schooling was meagre, and consisted largely of the study of mathematics and its practical application in surveying, a knowledge of which science was most useful in those early days of the conquest of the wilderness.

III. First Period of Career

1748–1775

Washington's active career may be said to begin just after his seventeenth birthday, with his employment by Lord Fairfax to survey the latter's vast estates in the wilderness beyond the Blue Ridge. There followed five years of varied experience; facing the hardships of the rough frontier life, travelling with his brother Lawrence, profiting by association with his accomplished friend and patron, Lord Fairfax, learning military tactics from two old soldiers at Mount Vernon, gaining business experience by settling the estate of Lawrence after the latter's death. In his diary, methodically kept during these years, we note the keen observation of men and incidents which stood him in such good stead later in life, as well as his clear and concise manner of relating his experiences. Contrary to the general belief, he was a careful reader at this time, laying the foundation of the knowledge of history and literature he later displayed, by reading English history and *The Spectator* from Lord Fairfax's library.

During the next five years, 1753–1758, this training Washington had been getting was put to the severest test. The events of this period had the greatest influence upon his later career. As commissioner from Governor Dinwiddie to the commandant of the French fort on the Ohio, he made his famous trip to the frontier through the unbroken forests of the Alleghanies, in great peril from flooded rivers and savage foes, travelling much of the return journey on foot and alone. As lieutenant-colonel of a militia company, he won his first battle. Surrounding a small French scouting party, he captured or killed all but one of its members. It was in writing of this battle that he said he loved to hear bullets whistle, a sentiment he afterwards considered as due to the folly of youth. He rashly continued the advance until nearly surrounded by a superior enemy, to whom, with more courage than wisdom, he offered battle in the open. His forces were finally defeated, and he was compelled to surrender his improvised fort, and retreat to the settlement.

His brilliant services in the ill-fated Braddock campaign are well known ; how he was everywhere in the hottest of the fight, how he had two horses shot under him and four bullets through his coat, how his courage and leadership rallied the remnants of the army and prevented its utter annihilation.

He was now made commander of all the Virginian forces, and spent many months on the frontier, trying to protect the widely scattered English settlers with an inadequate force, badly equipped and disorganized because of the incompetent management of the Virginia authorities. He finally joined the English force that occupied Fort Du Quesne after the withdrawal of the French, whose position had been made untenable by the success of the British in Canada.

The period thus closed shows the development of that strength of character and the military ability that were to make possible Washington's successful leadership in the Revolution. Into this struggle with the French and Indians the young colonial went a recklessly brave man, keen of observation, unsparing of himself; but rash and impetuous, despising his foes, impatient of delay, meeting bungling incompetence with an outspoken and harsh criticism that only increased his difficulties. Out of this school of experience he came a tried soldier and wise leader; his reckless bravery tempered with calm prudence, his impulsive nature held in check by a growing self-control. He had learned to bear with and to overcome the dullness and inefficiency of the government he served. With his habit of close observation, he had studied most effectively the European discipline of the British soldiers. He had learned to adapt his military art to circumstances and environment. Above all, he had discovered that British regulars were not invincible.

The seventeen years which follow, from 1758 to 1775, form, if a less stirring and picturesque, a hardly less important, period in Washington's training for the great crisis in his own and his country's career. He married, and settled down to the life of a country gentleman on his estates at Mount Vernon. He managed all the details of the plantation himself, keeping careful accounts. "He was a solid, square, evenly balanced man in those days. He farmed, as he fought and governed, better than anybody else." He was fond of outdoor life, and hunting was his favourite pastime. When he was forty, he could throw an iron bar farther than any competitor at the village sports. He was the best rider in Virginia. During these years Washington was a member of the Virginia House of Burgesses and of the Continental Congresses of 1774 and 1775 at Philadelphia. Patrick Henry said of him at this time: "If you speak of solid information and sound judgement, Colonel Washington is unquestionably the greatest man on the floor."

IV. Period of the Revolution

1775–1783

Congress having appointed Washington Commander-in-chief of the American army, he at once set out for Boston, and on July 3, 1775, under the historic elm at Cambridge, took formal command of the army amid a scene of great enthusiasm.

Various descriptions of General Washington at this time note his tall and well-proportioned figure and the nobility and majesty of his bearing, together with the modesty which marked his countenance.

The events of the next eight years of Washington's life are so well known that it would be superfluous to enlarge upon them here. However, it is well worth emphasizing that the history of our successful Revolution is the story of the self-sacrificing devotion to duty, the wise patriotism, and the supreme faith of its great leader and animating spirit, George Washington. His greatness is hardly appreciated until we realize that the actual direction of the campaigns and leadership of the army were perhaps the least of his arduous duties. It was Washington who practically planned and carried out the whole scheme of the colonial struggle. His hand is seen in every department of organization, even to the planning of the privateer service that carried the war to the shores of England. He had to provide the backbone and often the intelligence for a weak and irresolute Congress. Many times after a day of hard work he sat far into the night writing letters of entreaty, encouragement, or advice to Congress. His unflagging spirit and splendid perseverance in the midst of failure and discouragement were all that kept intact his ragged and half-starved army.

Defeated in the battles around New York in the autumn of 1776, many of which he was forced to fight for political effect against his own judgement, Washington made his masterly retreat across New Jersey, skilfully avoiding the pitched battles that would have annihilated his army and ended the Revolution. Never more resourceful than when in dire extremity, he closed this disheartening campaign, when British and Americans alike were daily expecting the end of the war, by the brilliant victories at Trenton and Princeton, thus safely passing the crisis of the Revolution.

The credit, not only for the conception and planning of these attacks, but also for their execution, belongs to Washington alone. The concerted action he had carefully worked out was prevented by the failure of his commanders to carry out their parts of the plan. Washington alone, undaunted by the winter storm of sleet and snow and by the ice-filled river, led his soldiers in person against Trenton. This campaign made a profound impression in Europe. Frederick the Great called it the most brilliant campaign of the century.

The war finally over with the surrender of Cornwallis at Yorktown, Washington took his memorable farewell of his officers at Fraunce's Tavern in New York. A few days later, on December 23, 1783, he surrendered his commission to Congress at Annapolis in a notable speech. He then retired to Mount Vernon, where he hoped to spend the rest of his days in the management of his estates amid the quiet country surroundings he loved.

V. Career as Statesman

1783–1799

In spite of this desire to give up public life, Washington soon found himself a leader in the movement for national union. As chairman of the constitutional convention at Philadelphia and as a member of the Virginia convention of ratification, his influence was the most powerful factor in the adoption of the Constitution and the establishment of the Union.

It was inevitable that Washington should be the first President of the new nation, and he was soon called by unanimous vote of the states again to take up the arduous duties of public office and leadership. Washington wisely judged that his first work as President must be the establishment of a strong central government that would command the respect and support of all the people, regardless of their state affiliations. Out of chaos he brought order and system. He originated the various departments that now constitute our federal government. He showed exceptional judgement in choosing a cabinet, selecting the ablest men who had supported the Constitution. He approved measures of Alexander Hamilton, his brilliant Secretary of the Treasury, that gave the young nation a financial standing among the powers and a sound basis of credit. Under Washington the principle of a tariff for the protection of home manufactures was first recognized and the internal revenue tax instituted.

Out of the attempt of the Scotch-Irish whiskey distillers in western Pennsylvania to evade the tax on whiskey, came the opportunity to establish the authority of the new central government. Washington exhausted every peaceful method of bringing these rebellious citizens to reason, and thus gained the support of all the rest of the country for his attitude toward the disaffected section. His efforts having proved futile, he raised an army of fifteen thousand men and put down the "Whiskey Insurrection" with such firmness and promptness as to impress upon all the people, not only that the new government could make laws for the welfare of the whole people, but also that it could enforce those laws.

More important even than his attitude in domestic affairs in establishing the nation securely was Washington's foreign policy. He insisted upon the doctrine of non-interference in European affairs as the only safe course for the struggling young nation to pursue. He thwarted every attempt of the over-zealous friends of the new French Republic to plunge America into the war between France and England. He demanded the settlement of differences between England and the United States growing out of the separation, even at some sacrifice to American pride, rather than run the risk of a war that might undo all the work of the Revolution. This attitude of non-participation in the war between France and England, and the terms of the Jay treaty with England, which were thought to be humiliating to America, brought upon Washington the severest criticism; and for a short time the blind partisanship of a part of the populace made him the most reviled man in the country. It is now clearly seen that both his domestic and foreign policies were essential to the successful establishment of the young nation. Again history clearly shows that America owed its successful induction into national life, as it did its independence, to the pre-eminent leadership of George Washington.

After publishing his Farewell Address in September, 1796, Washington retired to Mount Vernon. There he spent the last three years of his life in the simplicity of the home life he loved, and which he had denied himself for nearly a quarter of a century—not the least of the self-sacrifices Washington made for his country. On December 12, 1799, he took cold while riding over his plantation in a storm of sleet and snow. On the 14th he died peacefully and was buried in the family vault at Mount Vernon.

VI. Washington's Place in History

"When years after his death the world agrees to call a man great, the verdict must be accepted. The historian may whiten or blacken, the critic may weigh and dissect, the form of the judgement may be altered, but the central fact remains. . . . When we come to such a man as Washington, the case is still stronger. Men seem to have agreed that here was greatness which no one could question, and character which no one could fail to respect."

The nature and scope of the tributes paid Washington during the years since his death bear out this statement of Mr. Lodge's. Diplomat and general, poet and philosopher, all bear testimony to the supreme greatness of Washington. In the splendid monument erected to his memory at the Capital are inscriptions and tablets from every part of the civilized world, China and Siam and Greece vying with France and England in doing him honour.

Moreover, Washington's pre-eminence remains when we have stripped his character of the myths with which his boyhood was for so long surrounded, and of the cold and flawless grandeur with which his public career was invested by the formal descriptions of early biographers. The character of the real man Washington, as revealed by accurate and sympathetic historians like Henry Cabot Lodge and W. C. Ford, gains in power as we find that it was developed, like other strong characters, through struggles with very human traits of self-esteem, passion, and tempestuous temper. We may, therefore, feel secure in the conviction that George Washington is "the noblest figure that ever stood in the forefront of a nation's life."

THE COMPOSITION OF THE FAREWELL ADDRESS

In the preparation of the Farewell Address, Washington had the help of James Madison and Alexander Hamilton.

Having decided to retire to private life at the close of his first term as President, Washington justly felt that his services, coupled with the confidence in his judgement uniformly displayed by the people, warranted and compelled his giving to his countrymen, on the occasion of his retirement, the benefit of his advice on public questions. He was anxious that what he wrote should be so strongly and wisely expressed as to impress the people, and he wrote Mr. Madison asking him to draft a valedictory address to the public. Washington included in the letter the main points he wanted covered. Madison accordingly wrote out the first form of the Farewell Address.

Washington was finally persuaded to serve another term, and the address was not published. In 1796, when his second term was closing, Washington's determination to retire became fixed, and he reverted to the idea of a farewell address to the people. As he was not then on intimate terms with Madison because of differences in political views, he sent a copy of the original address, as amended by himself, to Hamilton for the latter's guidance in drafting a new farewell address. Hamilton made out headings for such a paper and may have written a complete address. This paper, in whatever form he received it, Washington worked over and amended in numerous places. In its final form the Address is therefore a composite paper, but in its spirit and its manner of expression it is the product of Washington's genius and character.

The Publication of the Farewell Address

The Farewell Address was published on Monday, September 19, 1796, in the Philadelphia *American Daily Advertiser*. The date usually assigned is the 17th of September, but the original manuscript in the Lenox Library, New York, is dated, "United States, 19th September, 1796." David M. Claypoole, editor and proprietor of the *Daily Advertiser*, states that the President sent for him a few days before the publication of the Address, told him of his intention to retire and of his desire to have published in the *Daily Advertiser* a farewell address to the people, which he had prepared. The date of publication was then agreed upon as the following Monday, September 19, and Washington dated the paper accordingly.

FAREWELL ADDRESS TO THE PEOPLE OF THE UNITED STATES

FRIENDS AND FELLOW-CITIZENS,

1. The period for a new election of a citizen to administer the executive government of the United States being not far distant, and the time actually arrived when your thoughts must be employed in designating the person who is to be clothed with that important trust, it appears to me proper, especially as it may conduce to a more distinct expression of the public voice, that I should now apprise you of the resolution I have formed, to decline being considered among the number of those out of[1] whom a choice is to be made.

2. I beg you, at the same time, to do me the justice to be assured that this resolution has not been taken without a strict regard to all the considerations appertaining to the relation which binds a dutiful citizen to his country, and that, in withdrawing the tender of service which silence in my situation might imply, I am influenced by no diminution of zeal for your future interest, no deficiency of grateful respect for your past kindness, but am supported by a full conviction that the step is compatible with both.

[1] What word should we now use?

3. The acceptance of, and continuance hitherto in, the office to which your suffrages[1] have twice called me, have been a uniform sacrifice of inclination to the opinion of duty and to a deference for what appeared to be your desire. I constantly hoped that it would have been much earlier in my power, consistently with motives which I was not at liberty to disregard, to return to that retirement from which I had been reluctantly drawn. The strength of my inclination to do this, previous to the last election, had even led to the preparation of an address to declare it to you; but mature reflection on the then perplexed and critical posture of our affairs with foreign nations and the unanimous advice of persons entitled to my confidence, impelled me to abandon the idea.

4. I rejoice that the state of your concerns, external as well as internal, no longer renders the pursuit of inclination incompatible with the sentiment of duty or propriety; and am persuaded, whatever partiality may be retained for my services, that in the present circumstances of our country you will not disapprove my determination to retire.

5. The impressions with which I first undertook the arduous trust, were explained on the proper occasion.[2] In the discharge of this trust, I will only say that I have, with good intentions, contributed towards the organization and administration of the government the best exertions of which a very fallible judgement was capable. Not unconscious, in the outset, of the in-

[1] Votes. [2] Washington's first inauguration.

feriority of my qualifications, experience in my own eyes, perhaps still more in the eyes of others, has strengthened the motives to diffidence of myself; and every day the increasing weight of years admonishes me more and more that the shade of retirement is as necessary to me as it will be welcome. Satisfied that if any circumstances have given peculiar value to my services, they were temporary, I have the consolation to believe that, while choice and prudence invite me to quit the political scene, patriotism does not forbid it.

6. In looking forward to the moment which is intended to terminate the career of my public life, my feelings do not permit me to suspend the deep acknowledgment of that debt of gratitude which I owe to my beloved country for the many honours it has conferred upon me; still more for the steadfast confidence with which it has supported me; and for the opportunities I have thence enjoyed of manifesting my inviolable attachment by services faithful and persevering, though in usefulness unequal to my zeal. If benefits have resulted to our country from these services, let it always be remembered to your praise, and as an instructive example in our annals, that under circumstances in which the passions, agitated in every direction, were liable to mislead, amidst appearances sometimes dubious, vicissitudes of fortune often discouraging, in situations in which not unfrequently want of success has countenanced the spirit of criticism, the constancy of

your support was the essential prop of the efforts, and a guarantee of the plans, by which they were effected. Profoundly penetrated with this idea, I shall carry it with me to the grave as a strong incitement to unceasing vows that Heaven may continue to you the choicest tokens of its beneficence, that your union and brotherly affection may be perpetual, that the free constitution, which is the work of your hands, may be sacredly maintained, that its administration in every department may be stamped with wisdom and virtue, — that, in fine, the happiness of the people of these States, under the auspices of liberty, may be made complete by so careful a preservation and so prudent a use of this blessing as will acquire to them the glory of recommending it to the applause, the affection, and adoption of every nation which is yet a stranger to it.

7. Here, perhaps, I ought to stop. But a solicitude for your welfare which cannot end but with my life, and the apprehension of danger natural to that solicitude, urge me on an occasion like the present to offer to your solemn contemplation, and to recommend to your frequent review, some sentiments, which are the result of much reflection, of no inconsiderable observation, and which appear to me all important to the permanency of your felicity as a people. These will be offered to you with the more freedom as you can only see in them the disinterested warnings of a parting friend, who can possibly have no personal motive to bias his counsels. Nor can I forget as an encourage-

ment to it your indulgent reception of my sentiments on a former and not dissimilar occasion.[1]

8. Interwoven as is the love of liberty with every ligament of your hearts, no recommendation of mine is necessary to fortify or confirm the attachment.

9. The unity of government which constitutes you one people, is also now dear to you. It is justly so; for it is a main pillar in the edifice of your real independence; the support of your tranquillity at home; your peace abroad; of your safety; of your prosperity in every shape; of that very liberty, which you so highly prize. But, as it is easy to foresee that from different causes and from different quarters much pains will be taken, many artifices employed, to weaken in your minds the conviction of this truth; as this is the point in your political fortress against which the batteries of internal and external enemies will be most constantly and actively (though often covertly and insidiously[2]) directed; it is of infinite moment that you should properly estimate the immense value of your national union to your collective and individual happiness; that you should cherish a cordial, habitual, and immovable attachment to it; accustoming yourselves to think and speak of it as of the Palladium[3] of your political safety and prosperity; watching

[1] Probably a reference to Washington's Circular Letter Addressed to the Governors of all the States on Disbanding the Army (1783).

[2] Secretly and treacherously.

[3] The image of Pallas in the citadel of Troy, on which the safety of the city was supposed to depend, hence safeguard.

for its preservation with jealous anxiety; discountenancing whatever may suggest even a suspicion that it can in any event be abandoned; and indignantly frowning upon the first dawning of every attempt to alienate any portion of our country from the rest, or to enfeeble the sacred ties which now link together the various parts.

10. For this you have every inducement of sympathy and interest. Citizens by birth or choice of a common country, that country has a right to concentrate your affections. The name of American, which belongs to you in your national capacity, must always exalt the just pride of patriotism more than any appellation derived from local discriminations. With slight shades of difference, you have the same religion, manners, habits, and political principles. You have in a common cause fought and triumphed together. The independence and liberty you possess are the work of joint councils and joint efforts, of common dangers, sufferings, and successes.

11. But these considerations, however powerfully they address themselves to your sensibility,[1] are greatly outweighed by those which apply more immediately to your interest. Here every portion of our country finds the most commanding motives for carefully guarding and preserving the union of the whole.

12. The North, in an unrestrained intercourse with the South, protected by the equal laws of a common government, finds in the productions of the latter great

[1] Emotions.

additional resources of maritime and commercial enterprise and precious materials of manufacturing industry. The South, in the same intercourse, benefiting by the agency of the North, sees its agriculture grow and its commerce expand. Turning partly into its own channels the seamen of the North, it finds its particular navigation invigorated; and while it contributes in different ways to nourish and increase the general mass of the national navigation, it looks forward to the protection of a maritime strength to which itself is unequally adapted. The East, in a like intercourse with the West, already finds, and in the progressive improvement of interior communications by land and water will more and more find, a valuable vent for the commodities which it brings from abroad or manufactures at home. The West derives from the East supplies requisite to its growth and comfort; and what is perhaps of still greater consequence, it must of necessity owe the secure enjoyment of indispensable outlets for its own productions to the weight, influence, and the future maritime strength of the Atlantic side of the union, directed by an indissoluble community of interest, as one nation. Any other tenure by which the West can hold this essential advantage, whether derived from its own separate strength, or from an apostate[1] and unnatural connexion with any foreign power, must be intrinsically precarious.

13. While, then, every part of our country thus feels an immediate and particular interest in union, all the

[1] False.

parts combined in the united mass of means and efforts cannot fail to find greater strength, greater resource, proportionably greater security from external danger, a less frequent interruption of their peace by foreign nations; and, what is of inestimable value, they must derive from union an exemption from those broils and wars between themselves which so frequently afflict neighbouring countries not tied together by the same government; which their own rivalships alone would be sufficient to produce; but which opposite foreign alliances, attachments, and intrigues would stimulate and embitter. Hence likewise they will avoid the necessity of those overgrown military establishments which, under any form of government, are inauspicious to liberty, and which are to be regarded as particularly hostile to republican liberty. In this sense it is, that your union ought to be considered as a main prop of your liberty, and that the love of the one ought to endear to you the preservation of the other.

14. These considerations speak a persuasive language to every reflecting and virtuous mind, and exhibit the continuance of the union as a primary object of patriotic desire. Is there a doubt whether a common government can embrace so large a sphere? Let experience solve it. To listen to mere speculation in such a case were criminal. We are authorized to hope that a proper organization of the whole, with the auxiliary agency of governments for the respective subdivisions, will afford a happy issue to the experiment. 'Tis well worth a fair and full experiment. With such powerful and obvious motives to

union, affecting all parts of our country, while experience shall not have demonstrated its impracticability, there will always be reason to distrust the patriotism of those who in any quarter may endeavour to weaken its bands.

15. In contemplating the causes which may disturb our union, it occurs as matter of serious concern that any ground should have been furnished for characterizing parties by geographical discriminations — Northern and Southern, Atlantic and Western ; whence designing men may endeavour to excite a belief that there is a real difference of local interests and views. One of the expedients of party to acquire influence within particular districts, is to misrepresent the opinions and aims of other districts. You cannot shield yourselves too much against the jealousies and heartburnings which spring from these misrepresentations ; they tend to render alien to each other those who ought to be bound together by fraternal affection. The inhabitants of our western country have lately had a useful lesson on this head. They have seen in the negotiation by the Executive, and in the unanimous ratification by the Senate, of the treaty with Spain, and in the universal satisfaction at that event throughout the United States, a decisive proof how unfounded were the suspicions propagated among them of a policy in the general government and in the Atlantic states unfriendly to their interests in regard to the Mississippi. They have been witnesses to the formation of two treaties, that with Great Britain and that with Spain, which secure to them every thing they could desire, in respect to our foreign rela-

tions, towards confirming their prosperity. Will it not be their wisdom to rely for the preservation of these advantages on the union by which they were procured? Will they not henceforth be deaf to those advisers, if such there are, who would sever them from their brethren, and connect them with aliens?

16. To the efficacy and permanency of your union, a government for the whole is indispensable. No alliances, however strict, between the parts can be an adequate substitute. They must inevitably experience the infractions and interruptions which all alliances in all times have experienced. Sensible of this momentous truth, you have improved upon your first essay, by the adoption of a constitution of government better calculated than your former[1] for an intimate union, and for the efficacious management of your common concerns. This government, the offspring of our own choice uninfluenced and unawed, adopted upon full investigation and mature deliberation, completely free in its principles, in the distribution of its powers uniting security with energy, and containing within itself a provision for its own amendment, has a just claim to your confidence and your support. Respect for its authority, compliance with its laws, acquiescence in its measures, are duties enjoined by the fundamental maxims of true liberty. The basis of our political systems is the right of the people to make and to alter their constitutions of government. But the constitu-

[1] The Articles of Confederation, under which the government operated from 1781 to 1788.

tion which at any time exists, till changed by an explicit and authentic act of the whole people, is sacredly obligatory upon all. The very idea of the power and the right of the people to establish government, presupposes the duty of every individual to obey the established government.

17. All obstructions to the execution of the laws, all combinations and associations, under whatever plausible character, with the real design to direct, control, counteract, or awe the regular deliberation and action of the constituted authorities, are destructive of this fundamental principle, and of fatal tendency. They serve to organize faction, to give it an artificial and extraordinary force, to put in the place of the delegated will of the nation the will of a party, often a small but artful and enterprising minority of the community; and, according to the alternate triumphs of different parties, to make the public administration the mirror of the ill-concerted and incongruous projects of faction rather than the organ of consistent and wholesome plans digested by common councils and modified by mutual interests. However combinations or associations of the above description may now and then answer popular ends, they are likely, in the course of time and things, to become potent engines, by which cunning, ambitious, and unprincipled men will be enabled to subvert the power of the people and to usurp for themselves the reins of government, destroying afterwards the very engines which have lifted them to unjust dominion.

18. Towards the preservation of your government and

the permanency of your present happy state, it is requisite, not only that you steadily discountenance irregular oppositions to its acknowledged authority, but also that you resist with care the spirit of innovation upon its principles, however specious [1] the pretexts. One method of assault may be to effect, in the forms of the constitution, alterations which will impair the energy of the system, and thus to undermine what cannot be directly overthrown. In all the changes to which you may be invited, remember that time and habit are at least as necessary to fix the true character of governments, as of other human institutions, that experience is the surest standard by which to test the real tendency of the existing constitution of a country, that facility in changes, upon the credit of mere hypothesis [2] and opinion, exposes to perpetual change from the endless variety of hypothesis and opinion; and remember, especially, that for the efficient management of your common interests in a country so extensive as ours, a government of as much vigour as is consistent with the perfect security of liberty is indispensable. Liberty itself will find in such a government, with powers properly distributed and adjusted, its surest guardian. It is, indeed, little else than a name, where the government is too feeble to withstand the enterprises of faction, to confine each member of the society within the limits prescribed by the laws, and to maintain all in the secure and tranquil enjoyment of the rights of person and property.

[1] Pleasing, or right and true, in appearance only. [2] Theory.

19. I have already intimated to you the danger of parties in the state, with particular reference to the founding of them on geographical discriminations. Let me now take a more comprehensive view, and warn you in the most solemn manner against the baneful effects of the spirit of party generally.

20. This spirit, unfortunately, is inseparable from our nature, having its root in the strongest passions of the human mind. It exists under different shapes in all governments, more or less stifled, controlled, or repressed; but in those of the popular form it is seen in its greatest rankness,[1] and is truly their worst enemy.

21. The alternate domination of one faction over another, sharpened by the spirit of revenge natural to party dissension, which in different ages and countries has perpetrated the most horrid enormities, is itself a frightful despotism. But this leads at length to a more formal and permanent despotism. The disorders and miseries which result, gradually incline the minds of men to seek security and repose in the absolute power of an individual; and sooner or later the chief of some prevailing faction, more able or more fortunate than his competitors, turns this disposition to the purposes of his own elevation on the ruins of public liberty.

22. Without looking forward to an extremity of this kind (which nevertheless ought not to be entirely out of sight), the common and continual mischiefs of the spirit

[1] Heavy growth of something disagreeable; as, of some unwholesome weed.

of party are sufficient to make it the interest and duty of a wise people to discourage and restrain it.

23. It serves always to distract the public councils, and enfeeble the public administration. It agitates the community with ill-founded jealousies and false alarms, kindles the animosity of one part against another, foments occasionally riot and insurrection. It opens the doors to foreign influence and corruption, which find a facilitated access to the government itself through the channels of party passions. Thus the policy and the will of one country are subjected to the policy and will of another.

24. There is an opinion that parties in free countries are useful checks upon the administration of the government, and serve to keep alive the spirit of liberty. This within certain limits is probably true, and in governments of a monarchical cast patriotism may look with indulgence, if not with favour, upon the spirit of party. But in those of the popular character, in governments purely elective, it is a spirit not to be encouraged. From their natural tendency, it is certain there will always be enough of that spirit for every salutary[1] purpose; and there being constant danger of excess, the effort ought to be, by force of public opinion, to mitigate and assuage[2] it. A fire not to be quenched, it demands a uniform vigilance to prevent its bursting into a flame, lest, instead of warming, it should consume.

25. It is important, likewise, that the habits of thinking in a free country should inspire caution in those entrusted

[1] Beneficial. [2] To make milder.

with its administration, to confine themselves within their respective constitutional spheres, avoiding in the exercise of the powers of one department, to encroach upon another. The spirit of encroachment tends to consolidate the powers of all the departments in one, and thus to create, whatever the form of government, a real despotism. A just estimate of that love of power and proneness to abuse it which predominates in the human heart, is sufficient to satisfy us of the truth of this position. The necessity of reciprocal [1] checks in the exercise of political power, by dividing and distributing it into different depositories and constituting each the guardian of the public weal against invasions by the others, has been evinced by experiments ancient and modern, some of them in our country and under our own eyes. To preserve them must be as necessary as to institute them. If, in the opinion of the people, the distribution or modification of the constitutional powers be in any particular wrong, let it be corrected by an amendment in the way which the constitution designates. But let there be no change by usurpation; for though this, in one instance, may be the instrument of good, it is the customary weapon by which free governments are destroyed. The precedent must always greatly overbalance in permanent evil any partial or transient benefit which the use can at any time yield.

26. Of all the dispositions and habits which lead to political prosperity, religion and morality are indispensable supports. In vain would that man claim the tribute of

[1] Mutual.

patriotism, who should labour to subvert these great pillars of human happiness, these firmest props of the duties of men and citizens. The mere politician, equally with the pious man, ought to respect and to cherish them. A volume could not trace all their connexions with private and public felicity. Let it simply be asked where is the security for property, for reputation, for life, if the sense of religious obligation desert the oaths which are the instruments of investigation in courts of justice? And let us with caution indulge the supposition that morality can be maintained without religion. Whatever may be conceded to the influence of refined education on minds of peculiar structure, reason and experience both forbid us to expect that national morality can prevail in exclusion of religious principle.

27. 'Tis substantially true that virtue or morality is a necessary spring of popular government. The rule indeed extends with more or less force to every species of free government. Who that is a sincere friend to it can look with indifference upon attempts to shake the foundation of the fabric?

28. Promote, then, as an object of primary importance, institutions for the general diffusion of knowledge. In proportion as the structure of a government gives force to public opinion, it is essential that public opinion should be enlightened.

29. As a very important source of strength and security, cherish public credit. One method of preserving it is to use it as sparingly as possible, avoiding occasions of

expense by cultivating peace, but remembering also that timely disbursements to prepare for danger frequently prevent much greater disbursements to repel it; avoiding likewise the accumulation of debt, not only by shunning occasions of expense, but by vigorous exertions in time of peace to discharge the debts which unavoidable wars may have occasioned, not ungenerously throwing upon posterity the burthen which we ourselves ought to bear. The execution of these maxims belongs to your representatives, but it is necessary that public opinion should co-operate. To facilitate to them the performance of their duty, it is essential that you should practically bear in mind that towards the payment of debts there must be revenue; that to have revenue there must be taxes; that no taxes can be devised which are not more or less inconvenient and unpleasant; that the intrinsic[1] embarrassment inseparable from the selection of the proper objects (which is always a choice of difficulties) ought to be a decisive motive for a candid[2] construction of the conduct of the government in making it, and for a spirit of acquiescence in[3] the measures for obtaining revenue which the public exigencies[4] may at any time dictate.

30. Observe good faith and justice towards all nations. Cultivate peace and harmony with all. Religion and morality enjoin this conduct, and can it be that good policy does not equally enjoin it? It will be worthy of a free, enlightened, and, at no distant period, a great na-

[1] Naturally belonging to; real.
[2] Frank.
[3] Acceptance of.
[4] Pressing necessities.

tion, to give to mankind the magnanimous and too novel example of a people always guided by an exalted justice and benevolence. Who can doubt that in the course of time and things, the fruits of such a plan would richly repay any temporary advantages which might be lost by a steady adherence to it? Can it be that Providence has not connected the permanent felicity of a nation with its virtue? The experiment, at least, is recommended by every sentiment which ennobles human nature. Alas! is it rendered impossible by its vices?

31. In the execution of such a plan, nothing is more essential than that permanent, inveterate antipathies[1] against particular nations and passionate attachments for others should be excluded; and that in place of them just and amicable feelings towards all should be cultivated. The nation which indulges towards another an habitual hatred or an habitual fondness, is in some degree a slave. It is a slave to its animosity or to its affection, either of which is sufficient to lead it astray from its duty and its interest. Antipathy in one nation against another disposes each more readily to offer insult and injury, to lay hold of slight causes of umbrage,[2] and to be haughty and intractable[3] when accidental or trifling occasions of dispute occur. Hence frequent collisions, obstinate, envenomed, and bloody contests. The nation prompted by ill will and resentment sometimes impels to war the government, contrary to the best calculations of policy. The government sometimes participates in the national propensity, and

[1] Hatreds. [2] Offence. [3] Unruly.

adopts through passion what reason would reject; at other times it makes the animosity of the nation subservient to projects of hostility instigated by pride, ambition, and other sinister[1] and pernicious motives. The peace often, sometimes perhaps the liberty, of nations has been the victim.

32. So likewise a passionate attachment of one nation for another produces a variety of evils. Sympathy for the favourite nation, facilitating the illusion of an imaginary common interest in cases where no real common interest exists, and infusing into one the enmities of the other, betrays the former into a participation in the quarrels and wars of the latter, without adequate inducement or justification. It leads also to concessions to the favourite nation of privileges denied to others, which is apt doubly to injure the nation making the concessions, by unnecessarily parting with what ought to have been retained, and by exciting jealousy, ill will, and a disposition to retaliate in the parties from whom equal privileges are withheld; and it gives to ambitious, corrupted, or deluded citizens (who devote themselves to the favourite nation), facility to betray or sacrifice the interests of their own country without odium,[2] sometimes even with popularity; gilding with the appearances of a virtuous sense of obligation, a commendable deference for public opinion, or a laudable zeal for public good, the base or foolish compliances[3] of ambition, corruption, or infatuation.[4]

[1] Evil.

[2] Without incurring the disgust of their fellow-countrymen.

[3] Yieldings.

[4] Extravagant fondness.

33. As avenues to foreign influence in innumerable ways, such attachments are particularly alarming to the truly enlightened and independent patriot. How many opportunities do they afford to tamper with domestic factions, to practise the arts of seduction, to mislead public opinion, to influence or awe the public councils! Such an attachment of a small or weak towards a great and powerful nation, dooms the former to be the satellite of the latter.

34. Against the insidious wiles of foreign influence, I conjure you to believe me, fellow-citizens, the jealousy of a free people ought to be constantly awake, since history and experience prove that foreign influence is one of the most baneful foes of republican government. But that jealousy, to be useful, must be impartial; else it becomes the instrument of the very influence to be avoided, instead of a defence against it. Excessive partiality for one foreign nation and excessive dislike of another, cause those whom they actuate to see danger only on one side, and serve to veil and even second the arts of influence on the other. Real patriots, who may resist the intrigues of the favourite, are liable to become suspected and odious; while its tools and dupes usurp the applause and confidence of the people, to surrender their interests.

35. The great rule of conduct for us, in regard to foreign nations, is, in extending our commercial relations, to have with them as little political connection as possible. So far as we have already formed engagements, let them be fulfilled with perfect good faith. Here let us stop.

36. Europe has a set of primary interests which to us have none, or a very remote relation. Hence she must be engaged in frequent controversies, the causes of which are essentially foreign to our concerns. Hence therefore it must be unwise in us to implicate ourselves by artificial ties in the ordinary vicissitudes[1] of her politics, or the ordinary combinations and collisions of her friendships or enmities.

37. Our detached and distant situation invites and enables us to pursue a different course. If we remain one people, under an efficient government, the period is not far off when we may defy material injury from external annoyance; when we may take such an attitude as will cause the neutrality we may at any time resolve upon to be scrupulously respected; when belligerent nations,[2] under the impossibility of making acquisitions upon us, will not lightly hazard the giving us provocation; when we may choose peace or war, as our interest guided by our justice shall counsel.

38. Why forego the advantages of so peculiar a situation? Why quit our own to stand upon foreign ground? Why, by interweaving our destiny with that of any part of Europe, entangle our peace and prosperity in the toils of European ambition, rivalship, interest, humour, or caprice?[3]

39. 'Tis our true policy to steer clear of permanent alliances with any portion of the foreign world; so far, I

[1] Ups and downs.

[2] Nations engaged in legitimate war.

[3] Whim.

mean, as we are now at liberty to do it; for let me not be understood as capable of patronizing infidelity to existing engagements. (I hold the maxim no less applicable to public than to private affairs, that honesty is always the best policy.) I repeat it, therefore, let those engagements be observed in their genuine sense. But in my opinion it is unnecessary and would be unwise to extend them.

40. Taking care always to keep ourselves, by suitable establishments,[1] on a respectably defensive posture, we may safely trust to temporary alliances for extraordinary emergencies.

41. Harmony, liberal intercourse with all nations, are recommended by policy, humanity, and interest. But even our commercial policy should hold an equal and impartial hand; neither seeking nor granting exclusive favours or preferences; consulting the natural course of things; diffusing and diversifying[2] by gentle means the streams of commerce, but forcing nothing; establishing with powers so disposed — in order to give trade a stable course, to define the rights of our merchants, and to enable the government to support them — conventional rules of intercourse, the best that present circumstances and mutual opinion will permit; but temporary, and liable to be from time to time abandoned or varied, as experience and circumstances shall dictate; constantly keeping in view that it is folly in one nation to look for

[1] Military and naval organization.

[2] Spreading abroad and varying.

disinterested favours from another; that it must pay with a portion of its independence for whatever it may accept under that character; that by such acceptance, it may place itself in the condition of having given equivalents for nominal favours, and yet of being reproached with ingratitude for not giving more. There can be no greater error than to expect or calculate upon real favours from nation to nation. 'Tis an illusion which experience must cure, which a just pride ought to discard.

42. In offering to you, my countrymen, these counsels of an old and affectionate friend, I dare not hope they will make the strong and lasting impression I could wish; that they will control the usual current of the passions, or prevent our nation from running the course which has hitherto marked the destiny of nations. But if I may even flatter myself that they may be productive of some partial benefit, some occasional good; that they may now and then recur to moderate the fury of party spirit, to warn against the mischiefs of foreign intrigue, to guard against the impostures of pretended patriotism; this hope will be a full recompense for the solicitude for your welfare by which they have been dictated.

43. How far in the discharge of my official duties I have been guided by the principles which have been delineated,[1] the public records and other evidences of my conduct must witness to you, and to the world. To myself the assurance of my own conscience is, that I have at least believed myself to be guided by them.

[1] Described.

44. In relation to the still subsisting war in Europe, my proclamation of the 22d of April, 1793, is the index to my plan. Sanctioned by your approving voice and by that of your representatives in both Houses of Congress, the spirit of that measure has continually governed me, uninfluenced by any attempts to deter or divert me from it.

45. After deliberate examination with the aid of the best lights I could obtain, I was well satisfied that our country, under all the circumstances of the case, had a right to take, and was bound in duty and interest to take, a neutral position. Having taken it, I determined, as far as should depend upon me, to maintain it with moderation, perseverance, and firmness.

46. The considerations which respect the right to hold this conduct, it is not necessary on this occasion to detail. I will only observe that, according to my understanding of the matter, that right, so far from being denied by any of the belligerent powers, has been virtually admitted by all.

47. The duty of holding a neutral conduct may be inferred, without anything more, from the obligation which justice and humanity impose on every nation, in cases in which it is free to act, to maintain inviolate the relations of peace and amity towards other nations.

48. The inducements of interest for observing that conduct will best be referred to your own reflections and experience. With me, a predominant motive has been to endeavour to gain time to our country to settle and

mature its yet recent institutions, and to progress without interruption to that degree of strength and consistency which is necessary to give it, humanly speaking, the command of its own fortune.

49. Though, in reviewing the incidents of my administration, I am unconscious of intentional error, I am nevertheless too sensible of my defects not to think it probable that I may have committed many errors. Whatever they may be, I fervently beseech the Almighty to avert or mitigate the evils to which they may tend. I shall also carry with me the hope that my country will never cease to view them with indulgence, and that after forty-five years of my life dedicated to its service with an upright zeal, the faults of incompetent abilities will be consigned to oblivion,[1] as myself must soon be to the mansions of rest.

50. Relying on its kindness in this as in other things, and actuated by that fervent love towards it which is so natural to a man who views in it the native soil of himself and his progenitors[2] for several generations, I anticipate with pleasing expectation that retreat in which I promise myself to realize, without alloy, the sweet enjoyment of partaking, in the midst of my fellow-citizens, the benign[3] influence of good laws under a free government, the ever favourite object of my heart and the happy reward, as I trust, of our mutual cares, labours, and dangers.

George Washington.

United States, September 17, 1796.

[1] Forgetfulness. [2] Ancestors. [3] Gracious.

OUTLINE OF WASHINGTON'S FAREWELL ADDRESS

Introduction

I. Washington's reasons for declining to be considered as a candidate for a third term as President.

- *A.* Sacrifice of personal inclination for retirement no longer demanded by public necessity.
- *B.* Growing conviction of personal need of retirement.

II. Washington's acknowledgment of his debt of gratitude to the country.

III. The counselling of his countrymen urged upon Washington by the occasion and by his solicitude for the welfare of the country.

Body

IV. Importance of unity of government.

- *A.* Value to the people of fixing the idea of national union in their minds.
- *B.* Material benefits of union to the sections of the country and to the country as a whole.
- *C.* Experience the proper test of the practicability of permanent union.

V. The danger to national unity of the geographical organization of parties.

VI. Respect for the Constitution essential to national unity.

VII. Baneful effects of the spirit of party.

- *A.* Autocracy the logical result of the disorders attendant upon party strife.
- *B.* Common and continual mischiefs resultant upon party spirit.
  1. Distraction of public councils and weakening of administration.
  2. Incitement of ill-founded jealousies and domestic quarrels.
  3. Subjection of the government to the danger of foreign influence and corruption.
- *C.* The defence of parties as checks upon government and supports of the spirit of liberty not applicable in governments purely elective.

VIII. Importance of keeping the departments of government separate in the exercise of their powers.

IX. Religion and morality, education and the maintenance of public credit, essential to political prosperity.

X. Attitude toward foreign nations.

- *A.* Observance of good faith and justice toward all nations.
- *B.* Avoidance of passionate hatreds and passionate attachments for any.
- *C.* Adherence to the principle of political independence of all.
- *D.* Cultivation of an impartial commercial intercourse with all nations.

Conclusion

XI. Summary of counsels and reaffirmation of Washington's purpose in offering them.

XII. Washington's attitude toward public questions determined by the principles he has recommended.

A. Adoption of a neutral position in the European war.

XIII. Acknowledgment of errors, and anticipation of the pleasures of private citizenship under the influence of free institutions.

GATEWAY SERIES

THE FIRST BUNKER HILL ORATION

OF

DANIEL WEBSTER

EDITED BY

FRANK W. PINE, M.A.

ENGLISH MASTER, THE HILL SCHOOL, POTTSTOWN, PA.

NEW YORK ∴ CINCINNATI ∴ CHICAGO

AMERICAN BOOK COMPANY

WEBSTER'S FIRST BUNKER HILL ORAT.

W. P. I

PREFACE BY THE GENERAL EDITOR

THIS series of books aims, first, to give the English texts required for entrance to college in a form which shall make them clear, interesting, and helpful to those who are beginning the study of literature; and, second, to supply the knowledge which the student needs to pass the entrance examination. For these two reasons it is called *The Gateway Series.*

The poems, plays, essays, and stories in these small volumes are treated, first of all, as works of literature, which were written to be read and enjoyed, not to be parsed and scanned and pulled to pieces. A short life of the author is given, and a portrait, in order to help the student to know the real person who wrote the book. The introduction tells what it is about, and how it was written, and where the author got the idea; and what it means. The notes at the foot of the page are simply to give the sense of the hard words so that the student can read straight on without turning to a dictionary. The other notes, at the end of the book, explain difficulties and allusions and fine points.

The editors are chosen because of their thorough training and special fitness to deal with the books committed to them, and because they agree with this idea of what a Gateway Series ought to be. They express, in each case, their own views of the books which they edit. Simplicity, thoroughness, shortness, and clearness, — these, we hope, will be the marks of the series.

HENRY VAN DYKE.

THE editor wishes to thank his friends and colleagues, Mr. Howard Bement, Dr. John A. Lester, and Mr. George D. Robins, for their valuable help in editing this book.

F. W. PINE.

THE HILL SCHOOL.

INTRODUCTION

LIFE OF DANIEL WEBSTER

In his life work and mission, Daniel Webster was a logical successor of George Washington. In his Farewell Address Washington gave to the American people, as the keynote of his work and his teaching, the idea of union and nationality. Webster took up this message and preached "the gospel of nationality throughout the length and breadth of the land." If Washington's prophetic vision first saw the necessity for creating a sentiment of nationality, it was Webster's life and words that fixed in the hearts of the American people the "fact of the Union" and the "principle of nationality."

Daniel Webster was born at Salisbury, New Hampshire, on January 18, 1782. His father, Ebenezer Webster, was descended from a long line of Scotch pioneers. He had been brought up on the frontier and had won the rank of captain in the French and Indian wars. In the Revolution he was a brave and efficient leader, whom Washington trusted. He was a man of powerful physique and strong character. From his mother, Abigail Eastman, Daniel Webster inherited his fine intellect.

As a boy Webster was weak of body but strong of mind. He had a remarkable memory and a talent for reading aloud. "Passing teamsters delighted to get 'Webster's boy,' with his delicate look and great dark eyes, to come out beneath the shade of the trees and read the Bible to them with all the force of his childish eloquence."

Webster was a simple, unaffected boy, neither forward nor precocious. He says of himself at this time that he loved reading and playing. Even as a boy he had the rare faculty of commanding the self-sacrificing devotion of those about him, and he returned this devotion with warm and affectionate gratitude.

Webster's preparation for college was poor. After spending nine months at Exeter Academy, he studied Latin and Greek with private tutors, but really knew little of either subject, and less of mathematics, geography, or history. It is noteworthy that while at Exeter this greatest of modern orators could not bring himself to declaim before his fellow-students.

At Dartmouth College, however, the qualities which afterward made Webster famous became apparent. He was the most eloquent speaker in college. "The gift of speech, the unequalled power of statement, which was born in him, just like the musical tones of his voice, could not be repressed. He was even then impressive. The boys about him never forgot the look of his deep-set eyes, or the sound of the solemn tones of his voice, his dignity of mien, and his absorption in his subject."

During his college course Webster was "studious, punctual, and regular in all his habits, and so dignified that his friends would as soon have thought of seeing President Wheelock indulge in boyish disorders as of seeing him do so. Yet with all his dignity and seriousness of talk and manner, he was a thoroughly genial companion, full of humour and fun and agreeable conversation. He was generally liked as well as universally admired, was a leader in the college societies, active and successful in sports, simple, hearty, unaffected."[1]

After his graduation in 1801, young Webster spent four years in the study of law in his native town and in Boston, where he was admitted to the bar. He began his practice of law in Boscawen, and after his father's death moved to Portsmouth, the principal town of New Hampshire. During this period of his Portsmouth practice, Webster was developing his powers as a pleader and public speaker.

Much of his "growth and improvement was due to the sharp competition and bright example of Jeremiah Mason, his chief opponent at the bar in these early days and one of the greatest common-lawyers in the country. Imitating Mason's plain, forcible style, Webster gradually rid himself of his florid, pompous manner of expression, and began to acquire the simplicity and directness which ended in the perfection of a style unsurpassed in modern oratory."[2]

During this period Webster had gradually entered politics as a moderate Federalist. As a result of his spirited opposition to the War of 1812 with England, he was elected to Congress. He took his seat in 1813 and remained in the House of Representatives until his election to the Senate in 1827, with an intermission

[1] H. C. Lodge, *Daniel Webster*. [2] Lodge.

of five years, spent in the practice of his profession in Boston, where he had removed in 1816. Mr. Webster soon showed his remarkable powers as a political speaker in his attacks upon the war policy of the government. He advocated a defensive war, a navy, and the giving up of the embargo or restrictions on our foreign commerce, so harmful to New England. He showed his strong love for the Union at this early date by declining to follow the extreme New England Federalists in their threats of secession if the war were not stopped.

Webster's most important service, perhaps, in his early career in Congress was his support of measures that gave us a sound currency and a safe medium of exchange. In his later Congressional career, Mr. Webster vigorously opposed a protective tariff. However, when New England had accepted the principle of protection and gone into protected manufactures, Webster ceased to oppose protection, but he never argued in its favour.

During the interim of five years between his terms in Congress, Mr. Webster argued the famous Dartmouth College Case, which gave him national fame as a lawyer. The free-thinking and ultra-liberal legislature of New Hampshire reorganized Dartmouth College, and the old orthodox Congregational and Federal Board of Trustees, who had their charter originally from the king, brought suit to set aside the new college organization. The case was carried to the Supreme Court, where Mr. Webster defended the College and its old board. He won the sympathy of the Federalist Chief Justice by a moving appeal to his religious and political prejudices. The Court sustained Mr. Webster's contention that the original charter of the college was a contract within the meaning of the Constitution, and as such could not be altered by a state.

It was also during this period of his private life in Boston, that Mr. Webster began the brilliant series of orations on public occasions, which made him the greatest occasional orator of his time. The first address of this nature was the oration at Plymouth in 1820, on the two hundredth anniversary of the landing of the Pilgrims, in connection with which John Adams wrote, "Mr. Burke is no longer entitled to the praise — 'the most consummate orator of modern times.'" The greatest of these addresses is undoubtedly The First Bunker Hill Oration. Others of nearly equal merit are the celebrated eulogy upon Adams and Jefferson, "The Character of Washington," the second Bunker Hill address, and the speech on laying the corner-stone for the addition to the Capitol, in 1851.

In 1827, with his election to the Senate from Massachusetts, began the last period of Mr. Webster's career as a statesman. Early in this period he reached the high-water mark of his power as a public speaker and statesman in his famous reply to Hayne, justly termed one of the greatest political speeches of all time. The speech also marks the highest point of his exposition of the fact of Union and the authority of the Constitution. Robert Y. Hayne of South Carolina had made a speech in the Senate giving the broadest interpretation to the Southern view, as expressed by his great leader, John C. Calhoun, that the Constitution was a compact and that any state had a right to declare a law passed by Congress which it considered unconstitutional, null and void within its borders. To this speech Mr. Webster made a crushing answer in what is popularly considered the greatest of his speeches, delivered on January 26–27, 1830. With powerful logic and clear and forceful expression, he expounded the view that the Constitution is the fundamental law of the land, and as such must be obeyed by the states. In words of burning eloquence he set forth the doctrine of nationality as opposed to that of state sovereignty. So ably did Webster defend these views that he insured their adoption by the great majority of the people of the country, who were thus prepared to support the principle of a Union one and indivisible, by force of arms when the issue was joined in less than ten years after Webster's death. Three years later, in reply to Calhoun's exhaustive defence of the doctrine of state sovereignty, Webster upheld the supremacy of the Constitution in what critics generally consider a more logical and conclusive, if less eloquent, argument, than his Reply to Hayne.

Had Mr. Webster's career closed at this point, he would stand as one of the greatest figures in our national history. As it is, his reputation suffered by his later seemingly inconsistent surrender to the slave power.

In his early speeches Webster had strongly denounced slavery as an institution, lamenting the necessity under the Constitution of permitting its continuance in the South. He had firmly resisted its extension, and he had been consistently opposed to any compromises on the question of extension. Toward the close of his career as senator his attitude on all three propositions seemed to change. Finally in 1850 he delivered his famous Seventh of March Speech. In this speech he virtually apologized for slavery as an institution, practically withdrew his opposition to its extension, and came out flatly for a compromise on the question of extension that was almost a surrender to the South. The speech caused widespread consternation and disgust among all who were opposed to slavery. Whittier wrote his poem *Ichabod,* castigating Webster for his desertion of the anti-slavery cause and bewailing the fall of a great moral force. Webster's friends soon rallied to his support, but his reputation never fully recovered from the blow it had received. That the Seventh of March Speech was a great mistake cannot be denied, that it was a deliberate surrender of principle may be very much doubted. The best explanation of Webster's conduct seems to be that in his passionate devotion to the Union he preferred a weak compromise to a breach between the states. He must have seen in 1850 that as things were going, war over the slavery question was inevitable. It seemed to him that the only way it could be averted was by one side or the other giving in. As he looked at the contending parties he felt instinctively that the South was by temperament, by tradition, and by its excellent political organization in no position to retreat on the question of the extension of slavery, so he determined to save the Union by weakening the anti-slavery party and so insuring a compromise.

Webster was twice Secretary of State; first in the cabinets of Presidents William Henry Harrison and his successor, John Tyler, from 1841 to 1843, and again in the cabinet of President Millard Fillmore, from 1850 until Webster's death in 1852.

As a diplomat his best known service is the negotiation of the Ashburton Treaty with England, which settled the northwestern boundary line between the United States and Canada.

Webster's great ambition was to be President, and from 1830 until his death he was a more or less prominent candidate for that office. But he was too great a statesman to be available as a party leader. His positive convictions and his great force in presenting them made him so many enemies that he was not a safe candidate. The mass of the people admired and respected his great ability, but they never loved him. His failure to attain the highest office in the nation embittered his last days. The loss of the Whig nomination in 1852 probably made easier the progress of a fatal disease that had already attacked Webster. He died at his home in Marshfield, near Boston, on October 14, 1852.

WEBSTER AS AN ORATOR

Daniel Webster is not only the greatest orator America has produced, he is one of the greatest orators of the world.

In keeping with his imposing presence, Webster's oratory was substantial and solid. In resonance and sonorousness, in directness and force, in eloquence of manner, in all the physical attributes of oratory, Webster was supreme. His manner was profound, weighty, sometimes heavy and inclining to pompousness. His argument was usually without ornament. He lacked the "poetic beauty and grace of Burke, the richness of imagery and language, but in clear, concise presentation and in direct force he was more effective than Burke. His appeal was to the intellect, the feelings, the memory, and interest of men, rather than to their imaginations. He possessed an unerring taste, a capacity for vigorous and telling sarcasm, a glow and fire none the less intense because they were subdued."[1]

Webster's great speeches, with the exception of the occasional orations, which were carefully written out, were usually prepared over night, but the material for them he had been storing up for years. When astonishment was expressed that he could make his famous reply to Hayne the next day after the latter's effort, he is said to have replied that he had been preparing for it all his life. His extraordinary memory and his ready command

[1] Lodge, *Daniel Webster*.

of learning made his mind a storehouse of knowledge, upon which he could draw at will. He was master of the art of effective arrangement of his material. Finally, he always saw the vital point of a case or a debate, an essential of successful debating. His style was dignified and sometimes bombastic after the manner of the early nineteenth century, but it was clear, concise, and forceful. He used some Latin derivatives, which lent themselves well to the sonorous and resonant tones of his powerful voice, but he preferred the simple Anglo-Saxon. His sentences were not long or elaborate. His speeches were well-rounded, finished productions.

THE BATTLE OF BUNKER HILL

The battle of Bunker Hill, June 17, 1775, was the first important engagement of the Revolution. At Lexington and Concord the embattled farmers had fired the shot heard round the world, and all New England had answered the call to arms. The American army had shut up the British in Boston and extended their lines in a semicircle of sixteen miles around the city from Jamaica Plain to Charlestown Neck. The only way to compel the evacuation of the city, which was the object of the Americans, was to seize the heights on the north and on the northeast. The New England Committee of Safety, having learned that General Gage had planned to extend his lines so as to cover Charlestown and Dorchester, at once sent a force of twelve hundred men under Colonel Prescott to fortify

Bunker Hill in Charlestown. The troops marched across Charlestown Neck to Bunker Hill at nightfall on June 16. After consultation here, it was decided to move on to what was later called Breed's Hill, which was connected by a ridge with Bunker Hill, and was an eminence affording better opportunity to annoy the town and the ships. Before the action the crest of Bunker Hill was also fortified as well as a rail fence to the left of the main redoubt on Breed's Hill. The next day, June 17, at noon the British troops began crossing the Charles River. At three o'clock they advanced in two columns to storm the entrenchments. "The scene was one long to be remembered. The tall grenadiers in brilliant uniform, their polished arms glistening in the midday sun, marching slowly but confidently up to the rudely constructed works, behind which the ill-dressed and half-awed 'rebels' stood, nervously handling their antiquated muskets; the continuous roar of the heavy guns from the batteries and the ships of war along the shore; the crackling of the flames ascending from the burning town; the thousands of spectators gathered on the house-tops and hill-sides to witness a conflict which might decide the fate of a continent,—all combined to make the scene one of unequalled grandeur and importance."

Under the wise orders of Prescott, Putnam, Stark, and Warren, the Americans held their fire until the British were within fifty yards, when suddenly they poured into the advancing lines such a deadly volley that the seasoned veterans wavered and finally fled down the hill. Another more determined attack met with the same repulse. The third attack, supported effectively by artillery, was successful, as the ammunition of the Americans became exhausted after a few volleys. The Americans finally retreated, but in fairly good order, leaving the entire heights to the English. During the retreat the Americans sustained their greatest loss in the death of General Joseph Warren, who was then the Chief Executive of Massachusetts and a recently appointed major-general. The British loss in killed and wounded was more than a third of the whole force engaged, including an unusually large proportion of officers. The American loss, mainly incurred during the final hand-to-hand struggle, was probably about one fourth of the whole force engaged. This destruction of life has rarely been exceeded in modern warfare.

While the British were victorious at Bunker Hill, the moral advantage of the battle was with the Americans. Both countries realized that the colonists could fight and that the task of subjugating the colonies would be a hard one. Vergennes, the French minister of foreign affairs, exclaimed that with two more such victories England would have no army left in America. Washington received news of the battle on his way north to take command of the colonial army. His first question was, "Did the militia fight?" On being told how bravely and stubbornly they defended their position, he said, "Then the liberties of the country are safe." Franklin declared that England had lost her colonies forever.

THE MONUMENT AND THE OCCASION

The first monument commemorating the Battle of Bunker Hill was that erected in 1794 by the Masons of Massachusetts to General Joseph Warren, who was Grand Master of the Masonic lodges in America at the time of his death.

The present Bunker Hill Monument was completed in 1843, when Webster delivered another commemorative oration. It is a granite shaft two hundred and twenty-one feet high and thirty feet square at the base. A spiral stairway winds up inside the monument to a circular chamber at the top. The complete cost of the erection and dedication of the monument was about $160,000.

As the semi-centennial of the engagement approached the Bunker Hill Monument Association was formed to erect a suitable monument to commemorate the battle itself. When the enterprise had so far proceeded that success seemed assured, it was determined to lay the corner-stone of the proposed monument on the fiftieth anniversary of the battle, June 17, 1825. The ceremonies were to be conducted by Daniel Webster, the President of the Association, assisted by the Grand Master of the Grand Lodge of Massachusetts Free Masons, and by General Lafayette, who was then on a tour of the states.

"This celebration was unequalled in magnificence by anything of the kind that had been seen in New England. The morning proved propitious. The air was cool, the sky was clear. At about ten o'clock a procession moved from the State House toward Bunker Hill. The military in their fine uniforms composed the van. About two hundred veterans of the Revolution, of whom forty were survivors of the battle, rode in barouches next to the escort. Some wore, as honourable decorations, their old fighting equipments, and some bore the scars of still more honourable wounds. To this patriot band succeeded the Bunker Hill Monument Association. Then the Masonic fraternity; then Lafayette, continually welcomed by tokens of love and gratitude, and the invited guests; then a long array of societies. It was a splendid procession, and of such length that the front nearly reached Charlestown Bridge ere the rear had left Boston Common. It proceeded to Breed's Hill, where the Grand Master of the Masons, the President of the Monument Association, and General Lafayette performed the ceremony of laying the corner-stone in the presence of a vast concourse of people." Prayer was offered by Rev. Joseph Thaxter, who, as the chaplain of Prescott's regiment in 1775, had offered a prayer for the American soldiers before the battle.

The oration was delivered from a platform erected on the northern slope of Breed's Hill overlooking the natural amphitheatre, then filled with twenty thousand people. On the platform with Mr. Webster were the Revolutionary veterans.

The imposing presence of the orator of the occasion as he rose before the great multitude formed a fitting climax to this impressive scene. "He seemed to every one to be a giant, and there is no better proof of his enormous physical impressiveness than this well-known fact, for Mr. Webster was not a man of extraordinary stature. He was five feet ten inches in height and, in health, weighed a little less than two hundred pounds. Wherever he went men felt in the depths of their being the amazing force of his personal presence. Every one is familiar with the story of the English navvy, who pointed at Mr. Webster in the streets of Liverpool and said, 'There goes a king.'" Carlyle's description in a letter to Emerson is almost as well known. "Not many days ago I saw at breakfast the notablest of all your notabilities, Daniel Webster. He is a magnificent specimen. The tanned complexion; that amorphous craglike face ; the dull black eyes under the precipice of brows, like dull anthracite furnaces needing only to be blown; the mastiff mouth accurately closed; I have not traced so much of silent, Berserkir rage that I remember of in any man."

"His voice was in harmony with his appearance. It was low and musical in conversation; in debate it was high but full, ringing out in moments of excitement like a clarion, and then sinking to deep notes with the solemn richness of organ tones, while the words were accompanied by a manner in which grace and dignity mingled in complete accord. The mere look of the man and the sound of his voice made all who saw and heard him feel that he must be the embodiment of wisdom, dignity, and strength, divinely eloquent."

THE BUNKER HILL MONUMENT

AN ADDRESS DELIVERED AT THE LAYING OF THE CORNER-STONE OF THE BUNKER HILL MONUMENT AT CHARLESTOWN, MASS., ON THE 17TH OF JUNE, 1825

I. 1. THIS uncounted multitude before me and around me proves the feeling which the occasion has excited. These thousands of human faces, glowing with sympathy and joy, and from the impulses of a common gratitude turned reverently to heaven in this spacious temple of the firmament, proclaim that the day, the place, and the purpose of our assembling have made a deep impression on our hearts.

2. If, indeed, there be anything in local association fit to affect the mind of man, we need not strive to repress the emotions which agitate us here. We are among the sepulchres of our fathers. We are on ground distinguished by their valour, their constancy, and the shedding of their blood. We are here, not to fix an uncertain date in our annals, nor to draw into notice an obscure and unknown spot. If our humble purpose had never been conceived, if we ourselves had never been born, the 17th of June, 1775, would have been a day on which all subsequent history would have poured its light, and the eminence where we stand a point of attraction to the eyes

of successive generations. But we are Americans. We live in what may be called the early age of this great continent; and we know that our posterity, through all time, are here to enjoy and suffer the allotments of humanity. We see before us a probable train of great events; we know that our own fortunes have been happily cast; and it is natural, therefore, that we should be moved by the contemplation of occurrences which have guided our destiny before many of us were born, and settled the condition in which we should pass that portion of our existence which God allows to men on earth.

3. We do not read even of the discovery of this continent without feeling something of a personal interest in the event; without being reminded how much it has affected our own fortunes and our own existence. It would be still more unnatural for us, therefore, than for others, to contemplate with unaffected minds that interesting, I may say that most touching and pathetic scene, when the great discoverer of America stood on the deck of his shattered bark, the shades of night falling on the sea, yet no man sleeping; tossed on the billows of an unknown ocean, yet the stronger billows of alternate hope and despair tossing his own troubled thoughts; extending forward his harassed frame, straining westward his anxious and eager eyes, till Heaven at last granted him a moment of rapture and ecstasy, in blessing his vision with the sight of the unknown world.

4. Nearer to our times, more closely connected with our fates, and therefore still more interesting to our

feelings and affections, is the settlement of our own country by colonists from England. We cherish every memorial of these worthy ancestors; we celebrate their patience and fortitude; we admire their daring enterprise; we teach our children to venerate their piety; and we are justly proud of being descended from men who have set the world an example of founding civil institutions on the great and united principles of human freedom and human knowledge. To us, their children, the story of their labours and sufferings can never be without its interest. We shall not stand unmoved on the shore of Plymouth while the sea continues to wash it; nor will our brethren in another early and ancient Colony forget the place of its first establishment, till their river shall cease to flow by it. No vigour of youth, no maturity of manhood, will lead the nation to forget the spots where its infancy was cradled and defended.

5. But the great event in the history of the continent, which we are now met here to commemorate, that prodigy of modern times, at once the wonder and the blessing of the world, is the American Revolution. In a day of extraordinary prosperity and happiness, of high national honour, distinction, and power, we are brought together, in this place, by our love of country, by our admiration of exalted character, by our gratitude for signal services and patriotic devotion.

II. 6. The Society whose organ I am was formed for the purpose of rearing some honourable and durable monument to the memory of the early friends of American Independence. They have thought that for this object no time could be more propitious than the present prosperous and peaceful period; that no place could claim preference over this memorable spot, and that no day could be more auspicious to[1] the undertaking than the anniversary of the battle which was here fought. The foundation of that monument we have now laid. With solemnities suited to the occasion, with prayers to Almighty God for his blessing, and in the midst of this cloud of witnesses, we have begun the work. We trust it will be prosecuted, and that, springing from a broad foundation, rising high in massive solidity and unadorned grandeur, it may remain as long as Heaven permits the works of man to last, a fit emblem, both of the events in memory of which it is raised, and of the gratitude of those who have reared it.

7. We know, indeed, that the record of illustrious actions is most safely deposited in the universal remembrance of mankind. We know, that if we could cause this structure to ascend, not only till it reached the skies, but till it pierced them, its broad surfaces could still contain but part of that which, in an age of knowledge, hath already been spread over the earth, and which history charges itself with making known to all future times. We know that no inscription on entablatures less broad than the earth itself can carry

[1] Timely for.

information of the events we commemorate where it has not already gone ; and that no structure, which shall not outlive the duration of letters and knowledge among men, can prolong the memorial. But our object is, by this edifice, to show our own deep sense of the value and importance of the achievements of our ancestors ; and, by presenting this work of gratitude to the eye, to keep alive similar sentiments, and to foster a constant regard for the principles of the Revolution. Human beings are composed, not of reason only, but of imagination also, and sentiment ; and that is neither wasted nor misapplied which is appropriated to the purpose of giving right direction to sentiments, and opening proper springs of feeling in the heart. Let it not be supposed that our object is to perpetuate national hostility, or even to cherish a mere military spirit. It is higher, purer, nobler. We consecrate our work to the spirit of national independence, and we wish that the light of peace may rest upon it forever. We rear a memorial of our conviction of that unmeasured benefit which has been conferred on our own land, and of the happy influences which have been produced, by the same events, on the general interests of mankind. We come, as Americans, to mark a spot which must forever be dear to us and our posterity. We wish that whosoever, in all coming time, shall turn his eye hither, may behold that the place is not undistinguished where the first great battle of the Revolution was fought. We wish that this structure may proclaim the magnitude and importance of that event to every class and every age. We wish that infancy may learn the purpose of its erection from maternal lips, and that weary and withered age may behold it, and be solaced by the recollections which it suggests. We wish that labour may look up here, and be proud, in the midst of its toil. We wish that, in those days of disaster, which, as they come upon all nations, must be expected to come upon us also, desponding patriotism may turn its eyes hitherward, and be assured that the foundations of our national power are still strong. We wish that this column, rising towards heaven among the pointed spires of so many temples dedicated to God, may contribute also to produce, in all minds, a pious feeling of dependence and gratitude. We wish, finally, that the last object to the sight of him who leaves his native shore, and the first to gladden his who revisits it, may be something which shall remind him of the liberty and the glory of his country. Let it rise! let it rise, till it meet the sun in his coming; let the earliest light of the morning gild it, and parting day linger and play on its summit.

III. 8. We live in a most extraordinary age. Events so various and so important that they might crowd and distinguish centuries, are, in our times, compressed within the compass of a single life. When has it happened that history has had so much to record, in the same term of years, as since the 17th of June, 1775? Our own Revolution, which, under other circumstances, might itself have been expected to occasion a war of half a century, has been achieved; twenty-four sovereign and independent States erected; and a general government established over them, so safe, so wise, so free, so practical, that we might well wonder its establishment should have been accomplished so soon, were it not far the greater wonder that it should have been established at all. Two or three millions of people have been augmented to twelve, the great forests of the West prostrated beneath the arm of successful industry, and the dwellers on the banks of the Ohio and the Mississippi become the fellow-citizens and neighbours of those who cultivate the hills of New England. We have a commerce that leaves no sea unexplored; navies which take no law from superior force; revenues adequate to all the exigencies of government, almost without taxation; and peace with all nations, founded on equal rights and mutual respect.

9. Europe, within the same period, has been agitated by a mighty revolution, which, while it has been felt in the individual condition and happiness of almost every man, has shaken to the centre her political fabric, and dashed against one another thrones which had stood tranquil for ages. On this, our continent, our own example has been followed, and colonies have sprung up to be nations. Unaccustomed sounds of liberty and free government have reached us from beyond the track of the sun;[1] and at this

[1] *I.e.*, from South America, where several republics had recently been established.

moment the dominion of European power in this continent, from the place where we stand to the south pole, is annihilated forever.[1]

10. In the meantime, both in Europe and America, such has been the general progress of knowledge, such the improvement in legislation, in commerce, in the arts, in letters, and, above all, in liberal ideas and the general spirit of the age, that the whole world seems changed.

11. Yet, notwithstanding that this is but a faint abstract of the things which have happened since the day of the battle of Bunker Hill, we are but fifty years removed from it; and we now stand here to enjoy all the blessings of our own condition, and to look abroad on the brightened prospects of the world, while we still have among us some of those who were active agents in the scenes of 1775, and who are now here, from every quarter of New England, to visit once more, and under circumstances so affecting, I had almost said so overwhelming, this renowned theatre of their courage and patriotism.

IV. 12. VENERABLE MEN! you have come down to us from a former generation. Heaven has bounteously lengthened out your lives, that you might behold this joyous day. You are now where you stood fifty years ago, this very hour, with your brothers and your neighbours, shoulder to shoulder, in the strife for your country. Behold, how altered! The same heavens are indeed over your heads; the same ocean rolls at your feet: but all else

[1] By the proclamation of the Monroe Doctrine.

how changed! You hear now no roar of hostile cannon, you see no mixed volumes of smoke and flame rising from burning Charlestown. The ground strowed with the dead and the dying; the impetuous charge; the steady and successful repulse; the loud call to repeated assault; the summoning of all that is manly to repeated resistance; a thousand bosoms freely and fearlessly bared in an instant to whatever of terror there may be in war and death; — all these you have witnessed, but you witness them no more. All is peace. The heights of yonder metropolis,[1] its towers and roofs, which you then saw filled with wives and children and countrymen in distress and terror, and looking with unutterable emotions for the issue of the combat, have presented you to-day with the sight of its whole happy population come out to welcome and greet you with a universal jubilee. Yonder proud ships,[2] by a felicity of position appropriately lying at the foot of this mount, and seeming fondly to cling around it, are not means of annoyance to you, but your country's own means of distinction and defence. All is peace; and God has granted you this sight of your country's happiness, ere you slumber in the grave. He has allowed you to behold and to partake the reward of your patriotic toils; and he has allowed us, your sons and countrymen, to meet you here, and in the name of the present generation, in the name of your country, in the name of liberty, to thank you!

13. But, alas! you are not all here! Time and the

[1] Boston.

[2] In the United States Navy Yard, at the base of the Hill.

sword have thinned your ranks. Prescott, Putnam, Stark, Brooks, Read, Pomeroy, Bridge! our eyes seek for you in vain amid this broken band. You are gathered to your fathers, and live only to your country in her grateful remembrance and your own bright example. But let us not too much grieve, that you have met the common fate of men. You lived at least long enough to know that your work had been nobly and successfully accomplished. You lived to see your country's independence established, and to sheathe your swords from war. On the light of Liberty you saw arise the light of Peace, like

> "another morn,
> Risen on mid noon;"

and the sky on which you closed your eyes was cloudless.

14. But ah! Him! the first great martyr[1] in this great cause! Him! the premature victim of his own self-devoting heart! Him! the head of our civil councils and the destined leader of our military bands, whom nothing brought hither but the unquenchable fire of his own spirit! Him! cut off by Providence in the hour of overwhelming anxiety and thick gloom; falling ere he saw the star of his country rise; pouring out his generous blood like water, before he knew whether it would fertilize a land of freedom or of bondage! — how shall I struggle with the emotions that stifle the utterance of thy name! Our poor work may perish; but thine shall endure! This monument may moulder away; the solid ground it

[1] General Joseph Warren.

rests upon may sink down to a level with the sea; but thy memory shall not fail! Wheresoever among men a heart shall be found that beats to the transports[1] of patriotism and liberty, its aspirations shall be to claim kindred with thy spirit!

15. But the scene amidst which we stand does not permit us to confine our thoughts or our sympathies to those fearless spirits who hazarded or lost their lives on this consecrated spot. We have the happiness to rejoice here in the presence of a most worthy representation of the survivors of the whole Revolutionary army.

16. VETERANS! you are the remnant of many a well-fought field. You bring with you marks of honour from Trenton and Monmouth, from Yorktown, Camden, Bennington, and Saratoga. VETERANS OF HALF A CENTURY! when in your youthful days you put everything at hazard in your country's cause, good as that cause was, and sanguine as youth is, still your fondest hopes did not stretch onward to an hour like this. At a period to which you could not reasonably have expected to arrive, at a moment of national prosperity such as you could never have foreseen, you are now met here to enjoy the fellowship of old soldiers, and to receive the overflowings of a universal gratitude.

17. But your agitated countenances and your heaving breasts inform me that even this is not an unmixed joy. I perceive that a tumult of contending feelings rushes upon you. The images of the dead, as well as the persons of the living, present themselves before you. The scene

[1] Emotions.

overwhelms you, and I turn from it. May the Father of all mercies smile upon your declining years, and bless them! And when you shall here have exchanged your embraces, when you shall once more have pressed the hands which have been so often extended to give succour in adversity, or grasped in the exultation of victory, then look abroad upon this lovely land which your young valour defended, and mark the happiness with which it is filled; yea, look abroad upon the whole earth, and see what a name you have contributed to give to your country, and what a praise you have added to freedom, and then rejoice in the sympathy and gratitude which beam upon your last days from the improved condition of mankind!

V. 18. The occasion does not require of me any particular account of the battle of the 17th of June, 1775, nor any detailed narrative of the events which immediately preceded it. These are familiarly known to all. In the progress of the great and interesting controversy, Massachusetts and the town of Boston had become early and marked objects of the displeasure of the British Parliament. This had been manifested in the act for altering the government of the Province, and in that for shutting up the port of Boston. Nothing sheds more honour on our early history, and nothing better shows how little the feelings and sentiments of the Colonies were known or regarded in England, than the impression which these measures everywhere produced in America. It had been anticipated, that while the Colonies in general would be terrified by the severity of the punishment inflicted on Massachusetts, the other seaports would be governed by a mere spirit of gain; and that, as Boston was now cut off from all commerce, the unexpected advantage which this blow on her was calculated to confer on other towns would be greedily enjoyed. How miserably such reasoners deceived themselves! How little they knew of the depth, and the strength, and the intenseness of that feeling of resistance to illegal acts of power, which possessed the whole American people! Everywhere the unworthy boon was rejected with scorn. The fortunate occasion was seized, everywhere, to show to the whole world that the Colonies were swayed by no local interest, no partial interest, no selfish interest. The temptation to profit by the punishment of Boston was strongest to our neighbours of Salem. Yet Salem was precisely the place where this miserable proffer was spurned in a tone of the most lofty self-respect and the most indignant patriotism. "We are deeply affected," said its inhabitants, "with the sense of our public calamities; but the miseries that are now rapidly hastening on our brethren in the capital of the Province greatly excite our commiseration. By shutting up the port of Boston, some imagine that the course of trade might be turned hither and to our benefit; but we must be dead to every idea of justice, lost to all feelings of humanity, could we indulge a thought to seize on wealth and raise our fortunes on the ruin of our suffering neighbours." These noble sentiments were not confined to our immediate vicinity. In that day of general affection and brotherhood, the blow given to Boston smote on every patriotic heart from one end of the country to the other. Virginia and the Carolinas, as well as Connecticut and New Hampshire, felt and proclaimed the cause to be their own. The Continental Congress, then holding its first session in Philadelphia, expressed its sympathy for the suffering inhabitants of Boston, and addresses were received from all quarters, assuring them that the cause was a common one, and should be met by common efforts and common sacrifices. The Congress of Massachusetts responded to these assurances; and in an address to the Congress at Philadelphia, bearing the official signature, perhaps among the last, of the immortal Warren, notwithstanding the severity of its suffering and the magnitude of the dangers which threatened it, it was declared that this Colony "is ready, at all times, to spend and to be spent in the cause of America."

19. But the hour drew nigh which was to put professions to the proof, and to determine whether the authors of these mutual pledges were ready to seal them in blood. The tidings of Lexington and Concord had no sooner spread, than it was universally felt that the time was at last come for action. A spirit pervaded all ranks, not transient, not boisterous, but deep, solemn, determined,

> "totamque infusa per artus
> Mens agitat molem, et magno se corpore miscet."

War on their own soil and at their own doors was, indeed, a strange work to the yeomanry of New England;

but their consciences were convinced of its necessity, their country called them to it, and they did not withhold themselves from the perilous trial. The ordinary occupations of life were abandoned ; the plough was stayed in the unfinished furrow ; wives gave up their husbands, and mothers gave up their sons, to the battles of the civil war. Death might come, in honour, on the field ; it might come, in disgrace, on the scaffold. For either and for both they were prepared. The sentiment of Quincy was full in their hearts. "Blandishments," said that distinguished son of genius and patriotism, "will not fascinate us, nor will threats of a halter intimidate; for, under God, we are determined that, wheresoever, whensoever, or howsoever we shall be called to make our exit, we will die free men."

20. The 17th of June saw the four New England Colonies[1] standing here, side by side, to triumph or to fall together ; and there was with them from that moment to the end of the war, what I hope will remain with them forever, one cause, one country, one heart.

21. The Battle of Bunker Hill was attended with the most important effects beyond its immediate results as a military engagement. It created at once a state of open, public war. There could now be no longer a question of proceeding against individuals, as guilty of treason or rebellion. That fearful crisis was past. The appeal lay to the sword, and the only question was, whether the spirit and the resources of the people would hold out till the object should be accomplished. Nor were its general conse-

[1] Massachusetts, Connecticut, New Hampshire, and Rhode Island.

quences confined to our own country. The previous proceedings of the Colonies, their appeals, resolutions, and addresses, had made their cause known to Europe. Without boasting, we may say, that in no age or country has the public cause been maintained with more force of argument, more power of illustration, or more of that persuasion which excited feeling and elevated principle can alone bestow, than the Revolutionary state papers exhibit. These papers will forever deserve to be studied, not only for the spirit which they breathe, but for the ability with which they were written.

22. To this able vindication of their cause, the Colonies had now added a practical and severe proof of their own true devotion to it, and given evidence also of the power which they could bring to its support. All now saw, that if America fell, she would not fall without a struggle. Men felt sympathy and regard, as well as surprise, when they beheld these infant states, remote, unknown, unaided, encounter the power of England, and, in the first considerable battle, leave more of their enemies dead on the field, in proportion to the number of combatants, than had been recently known to fall in the wars of Europe.

23. Information of these events, circulating throughout the world, at length reached the ears of one who now hears me. He has not forgotten the emotion which the fame of Bunker Hill, and the name of Warren, excited in his youthful breast.

VI. 24. SIR, we are assembled to commemorate the establishment of great public principles of liberty, and to do honour to the distinguished dead. The occasion is too severe[1] for eulogy of the living. But, Sir, your interesting relation to this country, the peculiar circumstances which surround you and surround us, call on me to express the happiness which we derive from your presence and aid in this solemn commemoration.

25. Fortunate, fortunate man! with what measure of devotion will you not thank God for the circumstances of your extraordinary life! You are connected with both hemispheres and with two generations. Heaven saw fit to ordain that the electric spark of liberty should be conducted, through you, from the New World to the Old; and we, who are now here to perform this duty of patriotism, have all of us long ago received it in charge from our fathers to cherish your name and your virtues. You will account it an instance of your good fortune, Sir, that you crossed the seas to visit us at a time which enables you to be present at this solemnity. You now behold the field, the renown of which reached you in the heart of France, and caused a thrill in your ardent bosom. You see the lines of the little redoubt thrown up by the incredible diligence of Prescott; defended, to the last extremity, by his lion-hearted valour; and within which the corner-stone of our monument has now taken its position. You see where Warren fell, and where Parker, Gardner, McCleary, Moore, and other early patriots fell with him. Those who

[1] Serious or solemn.

survived that day, and whose lives have been prolonged to the present hour, are now around you. Some of them you have known in the trying scenes of the war. Behold! they now stretch forth their feeble arms to embrace you. Behold! they raise their trembling voices to invoke the blessing of God on you and yours forever.

26. Sir, you have assisted us in laying the foundation of this structure. You have heard us rehearse, with our feeble commendation, the names of departed patriots. Monuments and eulogy belong to the dead. We give them this day to Warren and his associates. On other occasions they have been given to your more immediate companions in arms, to Washington, to Greene, to Gates, to Sullivan, and to Lincoln. We have become reluctant to grant these, our highest and last honours, further. We would gladly hold them yet back from the little remnant of that immortal band. *Serus in cælum redeas.*[1] Illustrious as are your merits, yet far, O, very far distant be the day, when any inscription shall bear your name, or any tongue pronounce its eulogy!

VII. 27. The leading reflection to which this occasion seems to invite us, respects the great changes which have happened in the fifty years since the Battle of Bunker Hill was fought. And it peculiarly marks the character of the present age, that, in looking at these changes, and in estimating their effect on our condition, we are obliged

[1] "May you return late to heaven."
HORACE, Book 1, Ode 2, 45.

to consider, not what has been done in our own country only, but in others also. In these interesting times, while nations are making separate and individual advances in improvement, they make, too, a common progress; like vessels on a common tide, propelled by the gales at different rates, according to their several structure and management, but all moved forward by one mighty current, strong enough to bear onward whatever does not sink beneath it.

28. A chief distinction of the present day is a community of opinions and knowledge amongst men in different nations, existing in a degree heretofore unknown. Knowledge has in our time triumphed, and is triumphing, over distance, over difference of languages, over diversity of habits, over prejudice, and over bigotry.[1] The civilized and Christian world is fast learning the great lesson, that difference of nation does not imply necessary hostility, and that all contact need not be war. The whole world is becoming a common field for intellect to act in. Energy of mind, genius, power, wheresoever it exists, may speak out in any tongue, and the *world* will hear it. A great chord of sentiment and feeling runs through two continents, and vibrates over both. Every breeze wafts intelligence from country to country; every wave rolls it; all give it forth, and all in turn receive it. There is a vast commerce of ideas; there are marts[2] and exchanges for intellectual discoveries, and a wonderful fellowship of those individual intelligences which make up the mind

[1] Obstinate attachment to a cause or creed. [2] Markets.

and opinion of the age. Mind is the great lever of all things; human thought is the process by which human ends are ultimately answered; and the diffusion of knowledge, so astonishing in the last half-century, has rendered innumerable minds, variously gifted by nature, competent to be competitors or fellow-workers on the theatre of intellectual operation.

29. From these causes, important improvements have taken place in the personal condition of individuals. Generally speaking, mankind are not only better fed and better clothed, but they are able also to enjoy more leisure; they possess more refinement and more self-respect. A superior tone of education, manners, and habits, prevails. This remark, most true in its application to our own country, is also partly true when applied elsewhere. It is proved by the vastly augmented consumption of those articles of manufacture and of commerce which contribute to the comforts and the decencies of life; an augmentation which has far outrun the progress of population. And while the unexampled and almost incredible use of machinery would seem to supply the place of labour, labour still finds its occupation and its reward; so wisely has Providence adjusted men's wants and desires to their condition and their capacity.

30. Any adequate survey, however, of the progress made during the last half-century in the polite and the mechanic arts, in machinery and manufactures, in commerce and agriculture, in letters and in science, would require volumes. I must abstain wholly from these subjects, and

turn for a moment to the contemplation of what has been done on the great question of politics and government. This is the master topic of the age; and during the whole fifty years it has intensely occupied the thoughts of men. The nature of civil government, its ends and uses, have been canvassed and investigated; ancient opinions attacked and defended; new ideas recommended and resisted, by whatever power the mind of man could bring to the controversy. From the closet and the public halls the debate has been transferred to the field; and the world has been shaken by wars of unexampled magnitude and the greatest variety of fortune. A day of peace has at length succeeded; and now that the strife has subsided and the smoke cleared away, we may begin to see what has actually been done, permanently changing the state and condition of human society. And, without dwelling on particular circumstances, it is most apparent, that, from the before-mentioned causes of augmented knowledge and improved individual condition, a real, substantial, and important change has taken place, and is taking place, highly favourable, on the whole, to human liberty and human happiness.

31. The great wheel of political revolution began to move in America. Here its rotation was guarded, regular, and safe. Transferred to the other continent, from unfortunate but natural causes, it received an irregular and violent impulse; it whirled along with a fearful celerity; till at length, like the chariot wheels in the races of antiquity, it took fire from the rapidity of its own motion,

and blazed onward, spreading conflagration and terror around.

32. We learn from the result of this experiment how fortunate was our own condition, and how admirably the character of our people was calculated for setting the great example of popular governments. The possession of power did not turn the heads of the American people, for they had long been in the habit of exercising a great degree of self-control. Although the paramount authority of the parent state existed over them, yet a large field of legislation had always been open to our Colonial assemblies. They were accustomed to representative bodies and the forms of free government; they understood the doctrine of the division of power among different branches, and the necessity of checks on each. The character of our countrymen, moreover, was sober, moral, and religious; and there was little in the change to shock their feelings of justice and humanity, or even to disturb an honest prejudice. We had no domestic throne to overturn, no privileged orders to cast down, no violent changes of property to encounter. In the American Revolution, no man sought or wished for more than to defend and enjoy his own. None hoped for plunder or for spoil. Rapacity was unknown to it; the ax was not among the instruments of its accomplishment; and we all know that it could not have lived a single day under any well-founded imputation of possessing a tendency adverse to the Christian religion.

33. It need not surprise us, that, under circumstances less auspicious, political revolutions elsewhere, even when

well intended, have terminated differently. It is, indeed, a great achievement, it is the master-work of the world, to establish governments entirely popular on lasting foundations; nor is it easy, indeed, to introduce the popular principle at all into governments to which it has been altogether a stranger. It cannot be doubted, however, that Europe has come out of the contest, in which she has been so long engaged, with greatly superior knowledge, and, in many respects, in a highly improved condition. Whatever benefit has been acquired is likely to be retained, for it consists mainly in the acquisition of more enlightened ideas. And although kingdoms and provinces may be wrested from the hands that hold them, in the same manner they were obtained; although ordinary and vulgar power may, in human affairs, be lost as it has been won; yet it is the glorious prerogative of the empire of knowledge, that what it gains it never loses. On the contrary, it increases by the multiple of its own power; all its ends become means; all its attainments help to new conquests. Its whole abundant harvest is but so much seed wheat, and nothing has limited, and nothing can limit, the amount of ultimate product.

34. Under the influence of this rapidly increasing knowledge, the people have begun, in all forms of government, to think, and to reason, on affairs of state. Regarding government as an institution for the public good, they demand a knowledge of its operations and a participation in its exercise. A call for the representative system, wherever it is not enjoyed, and where there is

already intelligence enough to estimate its value, is perseveringly made. Where men may speak out, they demand it; where the bayonet is at their throats, they pray for it.

35. When Louis the Fourteenth said, "I am the state," he expressed the essence of the doctrine of unlimited power. By the rules of that system, the people are disconnected from the state; they are its subjects; it is their lord. These ideas, founded in the love of power, and long supported by the excess and the abuse of it, are yielding, in our age, to other opinions; and the civilized world seems at last to be proceeding to the conviction of that fundamental and manifest truth, that the powers of government are but a trust, and that they cannot be lawfully exercised but for the good of the community. As knowledge is more and more extended, this conviction becomes more and more general. Knowledge, in truth, is the great sun in the firmament. Life and power are scattered with all its beams. The prayer of the Grecian champion,[1] when enveloped in unnatural clouds and darkness, is the appropriate political supplication for the people of every country not yet blessed with free institutions: —

> "Dispel this cloud, the light of heaven restore,
> Give me TO SEE, — and Ajax asks no more."

36. We may hope that the growing influence of enlightened sentiment will promote the permanent peace of the world. Wars to maintain family alliances, to uphold

[1] Homer's *Iliad*, Book xvii.

or to cast down dynasties, and to regulate successions to thrones, which have occupied so much room in the history of modern times, if not less likely to happen at all, will be less likely to become general and involve many nations, as the great principle shall be more and more established, that the interest of the world is peace, and its first great statute that every nation possesses the power of establishing a government for itself. But public opinion has attained also an influence over governments which do not admit the popular principle into their organization. A necessary respect for the judgement of the world operates, in some measure, as a control over the most unlimited forms of authority. It is owing, perhaps, to this truth, that the interesting struggle of the Greeks has been suffered to go on so long, without a direct interference, either to wrest that country from its present masters, or to execute the system of pacification by force, and, with united strength, lay the neck of Christian and civilized Greek at the foot of the barbarian Turk. Let us thank God that we live in an age when something has influence besides the bayonet, and when the sternest authority does not venture to encounter the scorching power of public reproach. Any attempt of the kind I have mentioned should be met by one universal burst of indignation; the air of the civilized world ought to be made too warm to be comfortably breathed by any one who would hazard it.

37. It is, indeed, a touching reflection, that, while, in the fullness of our country's happiness, we rear this monument to her honour, we look for instruction in our under-

taking to a country which is now in fearful contest, not for works of art or memorials of glory, but for her own existence. Let her be assured that she is not forgotten in the world; that her efforts are applauded, and that constant prayers ascend for her success. And let us cherish a confident hope for her final triumph. If the true spark of religious and civil liberty be kindled, it will burn. Human agency cannot extinguish it. Like the earth's central fire, it may be smothered for a time; the ocean may overwhelm it; mountains may press it down; but its inherent and unconquerable force will heave both the ocean and the land, and at some time or other, in some place or other, the volcano will break out and flame up to heaven.

38. Among the great events of the half-century we must reckon, certainly, the revolution of South America; and we are not likely to overrate the importance of that revolution, either to the people of the country itself or to the rest of the world. The late Spanish colonies, now independent states, under circumstances less favourable, doubtless, than attended our own Revolution, have yet successfully commenced their national existence. They have accomplished the great object of establishing their independence; they are known and acknowledged in the world; and although in regard to their systems of government, their sentiments on religious toleration, and their provisions for public instruction, they may have yet much to learn, it must be admitted that they have risen to the condition of settled and established states more rapidly

than could have been reasonably anticipated. They already furnish an exhilarating example of the difference between free governments and despotic misrule. Their commerce, at this moment, creates a new activity in all the great marts of the world. They show themselves able, by an exchange of commodities, to bear a useful part in the intercourse of nations.

39. A new spirit of enterprise and industry begins to prevail; all the great interests of society receive a salutary impulse; and the progress of information not only testifies to an improved condition, but itself constitutes the highest and most essential improvement.

40. When the Battle of Bunker Hill was fought, the existence of South America was scarcely felt in the civilized world. The thirteen little Colonies of North America habitually called themselves the "Continent." Borne down by colonial subjugation, monopoly, and bigotry, these vast regions of the South were hardly visible above the horizon. But in our day there has been, as it were, a new creation. The southern hemisphere emerges from the sea. Its lofty mountains begin to lift themselves into the light of heaven; its broad and fertile plains stretch out, in beauty, to the eye of civilized man, and at the mighty bidding of the voice of political liberty the waters of darkness retire.

VIII. 41. And now, let us indulge an honest exultation in the conviction of the benefit which the example of our country has produced, and is likely to produce, on human freedom and human happiness. Let us endeavour to comprehend in all its magnitude, and to feel in all its importance, the part assigned to us in the great drama of human affairs. We are placed at the head of the system of representative and popular governments. Thus far our example shows that such governments are compatible,[1] not only with respectability and power, but with repose, with peace, with security of personal rights, with good laws, and a just administration.

42. We are not propagandists.[2] Wherever other systems are preferred, either as being thought better in themselves, or as better suited to existing condition, we leave the preference to be enjoyed. Our history hitherto proves, however, that the popular form is practicable, and that with wisdom and knowledge men may govern themselves; and the duty incumbent on us is, to preserve the consistency of this cheering example, and take care that nothing may weaken its authority with the world. If, in our case, the representative system ultimately fail, popular governments must be pronounced impossible. No combination of circumstances more favourable to the experiment can ever be expected to occur. The last hopes of mankind, therefore, rest with us; and if it should be proclaimed, that our example had become an argument against the experiment, the knell[3] of popular liberty would be sounded throughout the earth.

[1] Things are *compatible* when they are capable of existing together.

[2] Those who propagate or spread abroad doctrines or systems.

[3] The sound of a bell that tolls slowly, as in the announcement of a death.

43. These are excitements to duty; but they are not suggestions of doubt. Our history and our condition, all that is gone before us, and all that surrounds us, authorize the belief, that popular governments, though subject to occasional variations, in form perhaps not always for the better, may yet, in their general character, be as durable and permanent as other systems. We know, indeed, that in our country any other is impossible. The *principle* of free governments adheres to the American soil. It is bedded in it, immovable as its mountains.

44. And let the sacred obligations which have devolved on this generation, and on us, sink deep into our hearts. Those who established our liberty and our government are daily dropping from among us. The great trust now descends to new hands. Let us apply ourselves to that which is presented to us, as our appropriate object. We can win no laurels in a war for independence. Earlier and worthier hands have gathered them all. Nor are there places for us by the side of Solon, and Alfred, and other founders of states. Our fathers have filled them. But there remains to us a great duty of defence and preservation; and there is opened to us, also, a noble pursuit to which the spirit of the times strongly invites us. Our proper business is improvement. Let our age be the age of improvement. In a day of peace, let us advance the arts of peace and the works of peace. Let us develop the resources of our land, call forth its powers, build up its institutions, promote all its great interests, and see whether we also, in our day and generation, may not per-

form something worthy to be remembered. Let us cultivate a true spirit of union and harmony. In pursuing the great objects which our condition points out to us, let us act under a settled conviction and an habitual feeling, that these twenty-four States are one country. Let our conceptions be enlarged to the circle of our duties. Let us extend our ideas over the whole of the vast field in which we are called to act. Let our object be, OUR COUNTRY, OUR WHOLE COUNTRY, AND NOTHING BUT OUR COUNTRY. And, by the blessing of God, may that country itself become a vast and splendid monument, not of oppression and terror, but of Wisdom, of Peace, and of Liberty, upon which the world may gaze with admiration forever!

OUTLINE OF THE FIRST BUNKER HILL ORATION

Introduction

I. Impression made on the audience by the occasion warranted by their interest in the accompanying circumstances.

- *A.* Their interest in the discovery of America.
- *B.* Their greater interest in the early settlement of America.
- *C.* Their greatest interest in the American Revolution, which they are gathered to commemorate at a time of extraordinary prosperity.

Body

II. Object of the erection of the monument.

- *A.* To show appreciation of the deeds of our ancestors, and to foster a constant regard for the principles of the Revolution.
- *B.* Not to perpetuate national hostility or to cherish mere military spirit, but to proclaim the benefits of the national independence to all mankind.

III. Important events since the Revolution.

- *A.* Progress of government and civilization in America.
- *B.* Revolutions in Europe and South America.
- *C.* General progress in Europe and America.
- *D.* Time of these occurrences brief, as shown in the presence of survivors of the Revolution.

IV. Address to the survivors of the battle, the dead leaders, and the veterans of the Revolution.

- *A.* Contrast between the fearful scene of the battle and the present peaceful prospect.
- *B.* Address to the dead leaders.
- *C.* Address to the martyr Warren.
  - 1. Endurance of his work and fame.
- *D.* Inclusion of other Revolutionary veterans present.
- *E.* Address to the veterans of the Revolution.
  - 1. Impossibility of their foreseeing their present happy situation.
  - 2. Tender of the sympathy and gratitude of fellow-men to add rejoicing to their other mingled emotions.

V. Review of the events leading to the Battle of Bunker Hill and of the effects of the battle.

- *A.* Unselfish unity of the colonies in support of Massachusetts and Boston against the coercive measures of the English Parliament.
- *B.* Uprising of the colonies in response to the tidings of Lexington and Concord.
- *C.* The New England colonies united at Bunker Hill.
- *D.* Effect of the Battle of Bunker Hill.
  - 1. Changing of uncertain rebellion to open war.
  - 2. Arousing of sympathy and regard of mankind for American cause.
  - 3. Exciting of sympathy of Lafayette.

VI. Address to Lafayette.

- *A.* Expression of happiness derived from his presence.
- *B.* Lafayette fortunate in being the transmitter of liberty from America to Europe and in his presence on this occasion.
- *C.* Wish of long life for Lafayette.

VII. Common progress of the nations since the Battle of Bunker Hill.

- *A.* The age distinguished by a community and diffusion of knowledge.
  - 1. Resultant improvement in the personal condition of individuals.
  - 2. Uplifting effect on government of these characteristics of the time.
- *B.* The political revolution in America and Europe contrasted.
  - 1. Americans better fitted for self-government.
  - 2. Improved condition of Europe from her revolutions in spite of their unhappy outcome.
- *C.* Result of increase of knowledge a universal demand among intelligent people for popular government.
- *D.* Doctrine of absolute monarchy giving way to the principle that government is a trust.
- *E.* Influence of enlightened sentiment in promoting peace and in checking arbitrary power.
  - 1. Non-interference in the Greek revolution an illustration.
- *F.* Hope and conviction of the ultimate success of the Greek revolution.
- *G.* The revolution in South America and its resultant uplift to that continent.
  - 1. Improved condition of society there.
  - 2. Contrast between position of South America at the time of Bunker Hill and its present position.

CONCLUSION

VIII. The influences of the example of the American experiment in popular government and the duty of Americans to insure the permanency of popular government.

- *A.* The practicability of popular government shown by present success of the American experiment.
- *B.* Duty of America to assure the permanent success of popular government.
- *C.* Probability of success of the American experiment.
- *D.* Duty of present generation of Americans to improve the country made independent and established by their fathers, and to cultivate the spirit of union.

NOTES

The heavy marginal figures stand for page, and the lighter ones for line.

WASHINGTON'S FAREWELL ADDRESS

22 : 11. **Perplexed and critical posture.** Cf. *Introduction*, p. 15. — 13. **Advice of persons.** Both Hamilton and Jefferson, leaders of rival parties and bitter opponents, as well as Madison and Randolph, urged Washington to accept another term because they were thoroughly alarmed at the prospect of a national conflict of parties. — 19. **Present circumstances of our country.** At the close of 1796 the government of the Union was well established. The credit of the country was assured by Hamilton's brilliant financial policy. The colonial spirit in American politics was giving way to a national spirit. Our foreign policy had been placed on a sound basis. The expansion of the West had been assured by the treaties with England and Spain. Our relations with foreign nations excepting France were satisfactory.

23 : 5. **Shade of retirement.** An example of the formal and artificial language peculiar to the later eighteenth-century writers. This diction is sometimes called "Johnsonese," from its greatest disciple, Dr. Samuel Johnson. Benjamin Franklin's style, as seen in the Autobiography, affords a good contrast to this heavy diction in its plain, homely language. Note other examples of this elevated diction as you read on. Is it in keeping with Washington's character and with the subject-matter of his address? — 9. **While choice and prudence.** Notice the excellent use of the balanced construction to summarize the contents of paragraphs 3–5. — 29. **Constancy of your support.** During the darkest days of the Revolution, when Washington's motives were questioned and his position attacked by the selfish and corrupt Conway-Gates Cabal, and later when as President he was bitterly maligned by political opponents, his leadership was never seriously threatened because of the unwavering support given him by the people, who thoroughly trusted his honesty and his wisdom.

24 : 17. **Here, perhaps, I ought to stop.** The introduction closes with paragraph 6. After a short transitional sentence, Washington states the theme of the Address in the second sentence of paragraph 7. From this sentence make as concise a title as you can.

25 : 6. **Importance of unity of government.** This is the first of the sentiments which Washington offers for consideration, paragraphs 9–14. Paragraph 11 is a good example of the transitional paragraph that helps to maintain the coherence of the whole theme; see also paragraph 19. — 15. **Political fortress.** Notice Washington's use of figurative language. The use of the metaphor, especially, is characteristic of the artificial style already commented upon. Do his figures of speech add to the clearness and force of the Address?

27 : 22. **Any other tenure.** The Kentuckians saw that the control of the Mississippi, then held by the Spaniards, was essential to their welfare. Having no sense of national responsibility, they were willing to become allies of France and send an army to drive out the Spanish. Washington saw the necessity for western expansion as clearly as did the frontiersmen, but his far-sighted plan was first to develop the resources of the Atlantic states, weld the country together, and let the march of events carry a united people to the inevitable conquest of the continent.

28 : 23. **Let experience solve it.** Washington, like Edmund Burke, his great English contemporary statesman, believed that all government should be based on experience and upon the constitution of the country. Cf. paragraphs 16–18.

29 : 5. Paragraph 15. Fundamental differences of political belief were already apparent between the New England and Middle

Atlantic states on the one hand and the South and West on the other. Even in recent years there have been attempts to create sectionalism, as in the free-silver discussion. — 27. **Two treaties.** The treaty with Great Britain secured the giving up of the frontier ports by the British, who, in violation of the articles of peace, had retained these outposts and used them as centres from which to instigate Indian warfare against the American pioneers. The treaty with Spain removed another western grievance by giving Americans the right to navigate the Mississippi, and by defining the southern boundary of the United States.

30 : 23. **Respect for its authority.** Note how the idea of respect for the Constitution is enforced in the rest of this paragraph by repetition in other words. In the next paragraph the same idea is further strengthened by pointing out the contrary evil effects of disobedience to constitutional government. Who was the great supporter of the Constitution and who were its ablest opponents during the next half century? Cf. *Introduction, Webster's First Bunker Hill Oration*, pp. 9–10.

31 : 7. **All combinations.** What organized attempts to nullify the Constitution can you mention?

32 : 19. **Government of . . . vigour . . . is indispensable.** The tendency in this country has been constantly to increase the powers of the federal government, and one of the important questions of the present time is how far the control of the central government over the business affairs of the nation shall extend.

33 : 5. **Baneful effects of the spirit of party,** paragraphs 19–24. While the author's statement of this topic makes it an exposition, it is in effect an affirmative argument on the question: Resolved, That in Democracies party spirit should be repressed. Outline Washington's argument. Notice the refutation in paragraph 24. — 13. **The alternate domination of one faction over another.** Illustrations of the evils here described may be found in both ancient and modern history. Perhaps the best example is afforded by the contentions of parties in the later Roman Republic.

These reached a climax in the great civil war between the aristocratic faction headed by Sulla and the party of the people led by Marius, 88–82 B.C. During this time no political change took place without bloodshed, and thousands of lives were sacrificed to party hatred. The final result was the downfall of the Republic and the dictatorship of Cæsar. The bloody factional strife of the latter part of the French Revolution undoubtedly proved the greatest factor in the elevation of Napoleon Bonaparte to the head of a French empire. Addison cites other examples of the evils of party spirit in one of the best of his *Spectator* papers (No. 125).

The principle of party government has been adopted in our own country from the beginning of our national career. Our President is of necessity a partisan. Even Washington, who avowed that he belonged to no party, was finally compelled to fill the chief administrative offices of the government with men who upheld his views on all public questions, in order to insure the carrying out of those views.

The legitimate function of the party in this country is to give voice to principles which the people believe to be for the best interest of the country, and by organized effort to enact those principles into law. The present danger from exaggeration of party spirit seems to be that party organization will be used to perpetuate party control of government for private ends without regard to principles or to the interests of the people.

35 : 2. **Avoiding . . . to encroach.** In the recent development of the power of the central government, the danger of Executive encroachment on the functions of the other departments has been pointed out as a real menace to constitutional government. One of the interesting questions now under discussion is the extent to which the Executive may go in interpreting the Constitution and the laws. One contention is that the President can only do for the general welfare what the law specifically permits him to do. The opposite view holds that the President may take any measures for the general welfare that the law does not specifically prohibit.

— 10. **Reciprocal checks.** Some of these are as follows: All treaties entered into by the Executive and all appointments made by him must be ratified by the Senate, while all bills passed by the House must be passed also by the Senate and signed by the Executive before they can become laws. The Supreme Court passes on the constitutionality of laws made by the legislative department.

If the conservative Executive and Senate had not had the power to carry through the Jay Treaty in Washington's Administration without the consent of the House, popular clamour would have declined the treaty and rushed us into a war with England that might have changed the destiny of the country at the very outset of its career.

35 : 19. **Corrected by an amendment.** Has it proved easy to amend the Constitution? How many amendments are there, and for what purposes were they made? What amendment is now proposed?

36 : 13. **Reason and experience both forbid.** Here and in the next paragraph the author is probably thinking of the unsuccessful attempts of the French revolutionists in 1793 to abolish religion, set up a Goddess of Reason, and establish national atheism.— 22. **Promote, etc.** In this connection it has been well said that as water cannot rise above its level, so a government cannot be better than those who establish it. Public education, both in its extent and its nature, is one of the important essentials of success in our experiment of free government.

37 : 2. **Timely disbursements.** This is the argument of those who advocate a great navy. A more pointed statement of the same idea is often quoted from a letter of Washington's: "There is nothing which will so soon produce a speedy and honourable peace as a state of preparation for war." — 20. **Spirit of acquiescence, etc.** Cf. *Introduction*, p. 15.

38 : 2. **Example of a people always guided by an exalted justice and benevolence.** The "Golden Rule" diplomacy of Secretary John Hay was based upon this principle. It gave us a greater influence in the settlement of the problems in China grow-

ing out of the anti-foreign agitation than was at all in keeping with our interests there. — 16. **Habitual hatred.** A reference to the general hatred of England then prevailing and the extravagant attachment to France.

40 : 21. **Real patriots.** This was exactly the case with Washington himself, when he resisted the intrigues of Genet, the French minister. See Lodge's *George Washington*, vol. ii, the chapter on Foreign Relations.

41 : 1. **Europe has a set of primary interests.** The Monroe Doctrine was based somewhat upon the ideas expressed in paragraphs 35–38. To what extent have we departed from the policy which Washington here so strongly recommends, and on what grounds is the departure defended ?

42 : 2. **Patronizing infidelity to existing engagements.** This refers to the obligations imposed by the existing treaties with Spain and England.

44 : 2. **My proclamation.** From the proclamation of neutrality in the war between France and England. "The duty and interest of the United States require that they should with sincerity and good faith adopt and pursue a conduct friendly and impartial toward the belligerent powers." France and Spain were both at war with England in 1796.

BIBLIOGRAPHY

Washington's Farewell Address

The standard edition of Washington's works is W. C. Ford's *Writings of Washington*, fourteen volumes.

The text of this edition of the Address follows Mr. Ford's reprint of the original, as contained in volume xiii of the *Writings*, pp. 277–279. Some slight changes have been made in the spelling, punctuation, and capitalization to make the text conform to modern usage.

Life

For the best brief life of Washington, see Henry Cabot Lodge's *George Washington*, two volumes, in the American Statesmen Series. Woodrow Wilson's *Life of Washington* gives a more informal and intimate picture of Washington and his times, and is excellently illustrated.

Critical Discussion

For a discussion of the composition of the Farewell Address consult Horace Binney's *Inquiry into the Formation of Washington's Farewell Address* or the *Forum*, vol. xxvii, p. 145.

A good history of the United States is essential to a proper study of the Farewell Address. Schouler's *History of the United States*, vol. i, is recommended.

NOTES

The heavy marginal figures stand for page, and the lighter ones for line.

WEBSTER'S FIRST BUNKER HILL ORATION

21 : 1. **This uncounted multitude.** We notice at once a fundamental difference between this oration and the Farewell Address. Webster is writing a speech to be delivered. Washington wrote for publication only. It will be interesting to note how the differing purposes compel a different handling of material. Webster's diction is simple and direct. He uses more short Anglo-Saxon words than Washington. The figurative language of Webster, as in "This spacious temple of the firmament," is used more to lend dignity and grandeur to the expression than clearness and force. Cf. paragraphs 8, 9, 31, 37, 40. While Washington frequently uses long sentences for explanation, Webster employs short incisive sentences. Washington repeats an idea in different words to explain and enforce his proposition, as on pp. 30 and 31 of the Address, while Webster uses a series of similarly constructed sentences with marked oratorical effect, as in paragraphs 2, 7, 44. Webster employs climax (paragraph 7) in a form that is most impressive in an oration, but that would seem out of place in the close exposition of the Address. Webster appeals to the feelings and interests of his hearers, as in these first few paragraphs and in 16 and 17 and 24 to 26. He presents the panorama of history with graphic vividness. He makes the veterans in his audience live over again with him the great scenes of the Revolution. There is life, action, feeling, throughout the oration. It moves rapidly yet with stately tread to its great moral exhortation at the close. Washington reaches the same end, the plea for national unity, by an appeal to the intellect, a less picturesque route, but one that served its purpose of influencing the entire country as well as the other did its aim of impressing a great audience gathered within hearing of the orator's voice.

23 : 12. **Plymouth.** The oldest New England town, where the Pilgrims landed, supposedly on the famous Plymouth Rock, December 21, 1620. Here on the 22d of December, 1820, Webster delivered the oration commemorating the two hundredth anniversary of the landing of the Pilgrims, the first of his occasional orations, and surpassed only by the First Bunker Hill Oration. — 13. **Another early and ancient Colony.** The Maryland Colony, established on the St. Mary's River in 1634, or the colony of Virginia, settled first at Jamestown on the James River in 1607; more likely the latter because Webster has coupled Plymouth and Jamestown in other speeches. — 27. **The Society.** Cf. *Introduction*, p. 17.

24 : 13. **Rising high.** Cf. *Introduction*, p. 17.

27 : 12. **Become.** The verb construction goes back to line 9; "have become" would be clearer. — 13. **We have a commerce.** Until ships were manufactured of iron, the merchant marine of the United States continued of the first importance because wooden ships could be built more cheaply in this country than anywhere else, while iron ships are built more cheaply abroad, and foreign-built ships cannot be registered in the United States. At present there are few sea-going ships of commerce flying the American flag. It has been proposed repeatedly to build up our merchant marine by government help, but the idea has not met with popular approval. — 20. **Mighty revolution.** The French Revolution, 1789–1804 (establishment of the empire). — 24. **On this, our continent.** Several of the Central and South American colonies of Spain had recently won their independence and established themselves as republics. — 27. **And at this moment.** The Monroe Doctrine, announced by President James Monroe in 1823, declared that the United States would consider any future attempt

of a European power, or combination of powers, to establish a colony or settlement on the American continents, or in any manner to control the destiny of the Spanish-American republics, as an unfriendly act. While this Doctrine has never been accepted in international law, its binding force has been tacitly admitted by the European nations. President Cleveland successfully invoked it against the threatened encroachments of Great Britain on Venezuelan territory in 1895, and in so doing made more definite the scope and terms of the policy.

28 : 14. **We still have among us.** The careful and natural transition from the review of events since the Battle of Bunker Hill to the address to survivors of the battle should be studied. The earlier Plymouth oration impresses one, as Webster's biographer, Mr. George Ticknor, says, as a series of eloquent fragments. The Bunker Hill Oration is not the less a succession of detached topics, but the rapidly perfecting art of the orator has so carefully welded these topics together that the continuity of the speech seems unbroken. Notice how this coherence of the whole theme is obtained by such transitional paragraphs and sentences as 15, first sentences of 18, 23, first sentence of 27. — 25. **Behold, how altered!** This paragraph and the two following are in Webster's best style. Paragraph 12 shows admirably his wonderful power of picturing historical scenes. Notice the short index sentence. Then follows a longer sentence, giving the background of the burning town. Now comes the central feature of the picture, the battle itself, with its rapid action, depicted by the short sentences in the same construction. The inclusive sentence "all is peace" makes an effective transition from the vivid scene of hurrying battle to the calm picture of repose and happiness, produced by the longer construction and the more quiet, dignified diction. The enforcement of the contrast by the repetition of "all is peace," the moving appeal to the feelings of the old soldiers, closing with the climax introducing the lofty sentiments of country, and liberty, serve as a fitting conclusion to the remarkable oratorical effect.

Paragraph 14 contains the celebrated apostrophe to General Warren. It seems as if the orator, carried away by his theme, turns to address the beloved patriot as if he were present. The result is a desirable impromptu effect.

30 : 12. Milton's *Paradise Lost*, Book V, ll. 310–311.

31 : 12. **Veterans!** Cf. *Introduction*, p. 18.

32 : 21. **Act for altering.** The King practically took control of the government of Massachusetts by assuming the right of choosing the members of the upper house of the legislature, by securing to the Royal Governor the right of appointing the judges and sheriffs and — through the sheriffs — the jurymen, and by prohibiting town meetings without the approval of the governor.

34 : 25. Virgil's *Æneid*, VI, 726: "A mind, pervading each limb, stirs the whole frame and mingles with the mighty mass." — Conington's translation.

35 : 8. **On the scaffold.** Patrick Henry's famous words are recalled, "Give me liberty or give me death," as well as the familiar quotation reputed to Franklin at the time of the signing of the Declaration of Independence, "Yes, we must indeed all hang together, or assuredly we shall all hang separately." — 9. **Quincy.** Josiah Quincy (1744–1775), American lawyer and patriot.

36 : 20. **Leave more of their enemies dead.** Cf. *Introduction*, p. 16. — 24. **One who now hears me.** General Lafayette. Cf. *Introduction*, pp. 17 and 18.

37 : 14. **From the New World to the Old.** Lafayette returned to France after the surrender of Cornwallis, and became one of the conservative leaders in the French Revolution. He was finally compelled to leave France in order to escape the consequences of opposing the excesses of the extreme revolutionists.

38 : 22. **The great changes which have happened in the fifty years.** This topic repeats the third somewhat. What difference do you notice between Webster's purposes in the two divisions of his oration? How differently does he treat the events he discusses here?

39 : 12. **Knowledge has . . . triumphed.** How was knowledge triumphing over distance in Webster's day? Can you think of any ways in which it is overcoming the other obstacles to world unity mentioned?

42 : 1. **Spreading conflagration and terror around.** The reference is to the violence and bloodshed accompanying the French Revolution, the principal features of which are detailed by the negative description of the American Revolution in the next paragraph. The ax spoken of in l. 24, p. 42, is the famous French guillotine, set up in the Place de la Concorde, Paris, which executed nearly three thousand persons between 1793 and 1795.

45 : 14. **Struggle of the Greeks.** The revolution of the Greeks against Turkey (1821–1828). It resulted in the independence of Greece. Lord Byron gave his services to Greece in this war and died of a fever during siege operations.

The great European powers have always taken a jealous interest in the affairs of Turkey and Greece, because these countries form the gateway to the East, and the powers are fearful lest anyone of their number should get control of that gateway.

47 : 8. **A new spirit of enterprise.** There is no paragraph here in the original speech as printed in 1825. Webster evidently thought one necessary when he revised the oration for publication with his other works in 1851. Was he right? — 19. **Has been.** In the original speech Webster said "hath been." Is the old verb form more in keeping with the poetic style of the paragraph? — 25. **And now, let us indulge.** Notice how easily Webster leads from the exposition of the spread of liberty and the consequent benefits to mankind to the lesson of his speech, the solemn obligation of Americans to preserve their inheritance of liberty and popular government, the keynote of which is national unity. Paving the way for his lesson, he appeals to the pride of his hearers by reminding them that the example of their country has produced these benefits, and that they stand at the head of the system of representative government. He follows this preparation by the

idea that this splendid prominence brings correspondingly great responsibility. A failure to preserve our liberty would doom popular government. Notice how this idea is expressed in such a way as to make his audience feel that they must not allow themselves to entertain for a moment a doubt as to the success of the experiment. This attitude of mind in the nation would be the greatest protection against disunion. Now he is ready for the conclusion. The foundations of liberty have been firmly laid, but on his hearers rests the solemn obligation of building a structure worthy of such a foundation. To them is open the splendid opportunity of assuring the permanence of popular government, and the orator closes with an appeal for national unity, which may have been intended even then as a veiled warning against the impending danger to the Republic of disunion.

48 : 18. **Fail.** Notice the use of the subjunctive to express doubt; an illustration of the contention that the subjunctive should be retained because it serves a useful purpose in expressing fine shades of meaning.

49 : 1. **Excitements.** *Incitements* would more exactly express the meaning here. — 19. **Solon, and Alfred.** Solon was the great Athenian law-giver, who reorganized the Athenian state on a liberal basis in 594 B.C. Alfred, surnamed "The Great," King of the West Saxons in England, from 871 to 901. By building improved ships and reorganizing the national militia, he drove the Danes out of England. He was a great scholar, and his administration was marked by judicial and educational reforms. "The services of Alfred to his people in peace and in war were so great that his fame has become almost as fabulous in legislation as that of Arthur in arms." — Hallam.

BIBLIOGRAPHY

Webster's Orations

The standard edition of Webster's works is that of Little, Brown and Co., published first in 1851. The *First Bunker Hill Oration* was originally published in pamphlet form by Cummings, Hilliard and Co., of Boston, in 1825, and ran through five editions in that year. The text here used is that of the oration as published in the *Works*, vol. i. This text was revised for publication by Webster, who improved the wording by slight changes.

Life

Daniel Webster, by H. C. Lodge in the American Statesmen Series.

The Life of Daniel Webster, by G. T. Curtis.

Encyclopædia Britannica, Ninth Edition, vol. xxiv.

Critical Discussion

"Webster as a Master of English Style," in E. P. Whipple's *Great Speeches of Webster*.

Century Magazine, September, 1893.

American Literature, Nichol.

History

Fiske's *American Revolution*, vol. i.

Bancroft's *History of the United States*, vols. iii, iv, and v.

Printed in the United States
128744LV00003B/44/A

9 781432 642549